LOVE

Karma

Use Your
INTUITION
to Find, Create,
and Nurture
LOVE
in Your Life

CHAR MARGOLIS

STERLING ETHOS
New York

STERLING ETHOS
New York

An Imprint of Sterling Publishing
387 Park Avenue South
New York, NY 10016

ISBN 978-1-4549-0664-3

Distributed in Canada by Sterling Publishing
c/o Canadian Manda Group, 165 Dufferin Street
Toronto, Ontario, Canada M6K 3H6
Distributed in the United Kingdom by GMC Distribution Services
Castle Place, 166 High Street, Lewes, East Sussex, England BN7 1XU
Distributed in Australia by Capricorn Link (Australia) Pty. Ltd.
P.O. Box 704, Windsor, NSW 2756, Australia

For information about custom editions, special sales, and premium
and corporate purchases, please contact Sterling Special Sales at
800-805-5489 or specialsales@sterlingpublishing.com.

Manufactured in the United States of America

2 4 6 8 10 9 7 5 3 1

www.sterlingpublishing.com

ACKNOWLEGMENTS

The journey of life is a treasure hunt. My love and gratitude to the treasures I have been blessed with: John Edward for his insight and encouragement, my sister Alicia Tisdale for her knowledge and wisdom, Vicki St.George for the nuts and bolts of the book, and Corinda Carfora for the icing on the cake. To Glynis McCants for her extraordinary talent in numerology, and Sandy Anastasi for her brilliant lessons in astrology. And especially to my parents for showing and teaching me the true meaning of a loving relationship: their own, and their love for our family. I am truly blessed.

CONTENTS

PREFACE

I've had a number of wonderful relationships in my life, as well as my share of painful ones. I know both the highs and lows of love intimately. I've also been very lucky to have seen the deep and lasting love between my parents (married for forty-six years before my dad passed over) as well as my sisters and their spouses (Elaine has been married to her husband, David, for over thirty-five years, and Alicia and Paul just celebrated their fifty-fourth anniversary). I've seen their mutual love become stronger as they have gone through the years together. My sisters and their husbands have seen the best and the worst in each other and it has only brought them closer. They are true examples of how love between partners can help people to grow and deepen their connection—not just with each other, but also with love itself. The lessons my sisters and their partners have taught me about love, sharing, kindness, unselfishness, and being separate yet united are some of the best guidance anyone could receive for creating great relationships.

Equally important, I have learned about the connection between love and psychic ability. Because of my work as a spiritual intuitive who has spent the last thirty-five years helping people get in touch with their loved ones on the other side, I know firsthand the power of love—not just on earth but for eternity. Love is the bridge that connects us all to the spirit world. It allows me to speak with those who have passed over, connecting deceased loved ones with those who are still here on earth. Love is the reason that most people come to me for a reading—they have lost someone dear to them and want to be reassured that their loved one is still present somewhere, safe and well. One recent example of this was Marinel, a woman who came to my television show for a reading. She had lost her mother when she was young and had had a difficult time—until she met the love of her life, Bernard. They married and began a wonderful life together, but their bliss was cut short when Bernard died in a car accident only a few years after their marriage. Marinel wanted to know if Bernard was okay on the other side. "We were together for such a short time, and we were so much in love," she said. "Is he at peace with the destiny that took him away so young?"

Like so many people who come to me for readings concerning their relationships, Marinel's story touched me deeply. As a spiritual intuitive, I can read the unique energies associated with different people both here and on the other side, and some energies are stronger than others. Marinel's husband Bernard came through very quickly and with very strong energy. "Bernard's saying there's nothing you could have done to prevent his death. It is the way it is," I told Marinel. "He's also saying that you gave him the greatest gift, because he lived long enough to know what it is to really feel love and be in love with someone else. He never was in love with anyone else but you. And it's the same for you—the hard part is that you're still here while he's in heaven."

As I continued speaking, Marinel's eyes glistened with tears. "He's saying that you put something in his hand before he died.

I can't see it because he's still holding it clenched in his fist. He says that no one knows you gave him this, but it will be with him forever."

Marinel looked at me in shock. "Before my mother died she gave me a chestnut. It was a little thing, but it meant a lot to me. Before Bernard died I gave him that chestnut. No one knew about it but me." I smiled.

"The funny thing was that the day before Bernard was cremated, a little girl went into my brother's garden, picked a chestnut, and gave it to me," Marinel said. "She told me, 'That's for you.' She didn't know about my mother's chestnut, but I thought that maybe Bernard asked her to give it to me as a sign from him."

"I'm sure you're right," I told her. "It was a sign that he still loves you and is with you and always will be. And when you go to heaven many years from now, Bernard will be there to welcome you home."

In this book you'll learn how you can use your intuition to help you find and deepen your intimate relationships, so you can continue to learn the lessons of love that you came to earth to master. Learn how to use the power of your intuition—along with logic, communication, and common sense—to help you create loving, fulfilling relationships that will enrich your life here on earth and on the other side.

Of all fires,
LOVE
is the only
inexhaustible
one.

Pablo Neruda

What's Love Got to Do with It?

We've all felt it, or wanted it: that feeling of overwhelming, all-encompassing love that sweeps us off our feet and raises us up to the heights of ecstasy. We've read about, and per-haps experienced, moments when we gazed into the eyes of another person and felt as if we were looking into the soul of someone closer to us than any other human being on earth. When we are in love, we feel that we're connected on every level: physically, mentally, emotionally, spiritually. It's as if we've known this person forever. We finish each other's sentences. We spend hours in each other's company. We constantly call or text or IM our beloved. When we sit in a meeting or wait in line at a store and hear our lover's special ring or the beep of an incoming message, our heart beats a little faster. Without a shadow of a doubt, we know that this love was meant to be. Any barriers or obstacles are simply tests of our commitment to each other. We can't imagine how we lived before we met this special someone, and we can't imagine living without them now that they have come into our lives.

Unfortunately, most of us also have had the flip side, when we've "lost that lovin' feeling." As much as love's ecstasy can lift us to the clouds, it can lead to a devastating fall. Maybe it's cooled down, went bad, or just fizzled out. Usually reality has stepped in and changed the music: our "perfect" beloved turns out to be human with feet, legs, and a head of clay. Suddenly we are faced with issues dealing with family, children, and jobs. Throw in a few bad habits, irresponsibility, messed-up finances, and the ever-popular "socks on the floor," and suddenly the perfect relationship becomes a bad sitcom.

Or, over the days, months, or years, our attraction to our lover slowly evaporates. The good points seem to fade into the mist, leaving only the top of the empty toothpaste tube in high def: we start to see only the bad things.

Of course there are far worse trials to experience: betrayal, addiction, compulsive behavior, abandonment, and violence. And even if we have the perfect partner, eventually our beloved can be snatched away by disease or death. The beautiful love we thought would last forever seems to vanish, leaving in its place heartache, regret, and despair. In some cases we find ourselves chasing after our lover, desperately hoping to rekindle the passion in them that we are still feeling. Yes, the loss of that special love can create some of the worst feelings in our lives. But relationships are why we are here: to experience them and share love.

Intimate relationships are the source of our greatest joy and greatest pain because they allow us to learn about love—and love is the strongest power in the universe. We all are born with the need to give and receive love. Our whole purpose on earth is to learn and grow in our ability to love and be loved, and the purpose of relationships is to teach our souls to love deeply and well.

Indeed, our relationships are magnifiers; they are the perfect mirror in which we see our strengths and weaknesses played out in front of us. We learn more about ourselves through relationships than we could in any other way—that's the other reason that they are such an important part of our soul's journey here on earth as well as the other side. Relationships put our concept of who we are to the test: it's a self-challenge that we're not always aware of. We're kind, loving, compassionate beings—except when our sweetie makes us angry! However, it's in our closest relationships that we learn the most about loving and being loved.

Good relationships teach us about God and divine love because they connect us to the Divine in a more personal way. By understanding this deep personal connection, we can then begin to understand how important it is to carry this depth into the realm of our physical world where we interact with people—our loved ones. A heavenly relationship here on earth is the closest we will come to feeling one with love. Conversely, a bad relationship teaches us more than we would ever want to know about hell.

So what's love got to do with it? Everything...

CHAPTER 1

The Good, the Bad, and the Ugly

Many of our relationships—and, I believe, all of our important *relationships*—extend far beyond our current lifetime on earth. Our loving relationships exist before we come into this life, and they will continue after we pass over. The people we choose for our relationships are our greatest teachers and we are theirs in return. As we see the grace and perfection in our partner, we are better able to experience those qualities in our lives. Learning to create deep relationships with another soul is one of the core reasons we come to earth, and if we don't learn certain lessons during this lifetime we're destined to repeat them...regardless of whether or not it's in THIS lifetime.

Most of us have experienced the good, the bad, and the ugly, and sometimes it seems like there's more bad and ugly than good. But the lessons we learn in relationships can be more painful than they really need to be: it's like the universe giving us a smack in the head. I am willing to bet that most of us instinctively know when things are going wrong, but our emotions, our fears, and our intellect keep us from making the true and right decisions (*gee, I put so much time into this relationship I can't bail now*). Love is kind of like the little girl in the Longfellow poem: "When she was good, she was very, very good, but when she was bad, she was horrid." Our mission is to experience more of the good and less of the bad. Don't misunderstand: we will never eliminate bad relationships—we need them to learn and grow. But our experience with bad relationships can be made less painful. What if we could find the partners who are best for us while avoiding the ones who might cause us unnecessary pain? What if we could enjoy our relationships and make them closer and deeper? And what if we could have not just the faith but the actual experience of maintaining our loving connection with our partners, even when we are divided by death? Once we heighten our awareness, we can become better at recognizing whether or not a relationship is going to help us flourish...or whether it will become toxic.

That's where our God-given sixth sense, or intuition, comes into play. My life's mission and my goal is to help people develop their inner wisdom, that inborn sense of "knowing" that can guide their lives. I hope that becomes your goal as well. People are given intuition to help them make better choices and prevent problems. This is particularly true when it comes to relationships.

Intuition can point us to the party or the street corner or the office where we "accidentally" bump into the person we fall madly in love with. We get a hunch to walk down a certain street or go into a local restaurant. Something compels us to move in a particular direction. That is our intuition—our inner compass. And it can give us the inner certainty that *this* is the person we are destined to marry.

In a great relationship, love and intuition can work hand-in-hand to create strong connections and bonds between partners. If there are potential problems, intuition can sometimes warn us in advance so we can prevent them. Or intuition can act as a cosmic smoke alarm, signaling a serious problem before we actually see the fire that is destroying the house of our relationship. Often clients tell me there's "something bothering them." They may have no reason for concern, but something in their relationship feels off. "He told me he was going out of town for a business trip, but I can't shake the feeling he's not going alone," a woman might say. Or a man might tell me, "I was lying next to my girlfriend in bed this weekend, she was asleep, and all of a sudden the thought popped into my head: 'She's been seeing someone else.' I've never thought such a thing before!"

When we understand our intuition and pay attention to its promptings, it can help us create the rich, deep, healthy, loving relationships we deserve. It can help us learn painful lessons more quickly, and it can show us how to move on to better relationships.

Remember that **intuition guides us. But it cannot stop us from going through the lessons we were born to learn this time around.**

Life on earth is like a school, and we are born so we can make progress and learn how to love. And at the core of our experience always lies the one question: How well did we love? Did we grow in our ability to give and receive love? Did we become more like our divine nature—the truth of who we are, which is like God? When we begin to approach our divine nature, we get closer to our own highest level of goodness, love, and wisdom. That is the true goal of our existence and of all our relationships: to become more loving of ourselves, of other beings, and of God. And that's the real experience we seek in our intimate relationships: that feeling of connection to ourselves, to another soul, and to the divine. Intuition can help us find, create, and nurture the kind of rich, wonderful, inspiring, and fulfilling relationships that make our souls sing, both here and in the hereafter.

Connecting with a Partner through INTUITION

Each day is a new adventure in discovering relationships—both the great ones and the not-so-great ones. The people who come to me for readings often want to know one of five things:

1. "My partner has passed over—is he okay? Does he still love me?"

2. "I'm in a new relationship—do my friends, relatives, and former partners on the other side approve?"

3. "Is there anything going on that I don't know about with my partner, such as an affair or other secrets that could threaten our relationship?"

4. "Is this new love right for me? Is he my soul mate? What do I need to know about him?"

5. "When will I meet Mr. or Ms. Right?"

In answering all these questions, I am constantly reminded that everyone has a unique energy. Each of us has what I call an energy "thumbprint," a vibration that is exclusive to our individual personality. It's what lets you know when a loved one enters the room even if you can't see them—you FEEL their presence. It is the same when people pass over; their spirits retain that unique energy on the other side, which we will always recognize regardless of where we are, because our love draws them to us.

I feel very fortunate that I have an uncommon sensitivity and am able to tune in to these energies, but in reality, each of us can do it. Really! It's a matter of practice and recognizing the signs. I do caution that if you decide to seek psychic counseling, please do your homework. Check with other clients; check if the psychic has a website or a newsletter. Be sure you are dealing with someone credible. Once you find that person, be prepared to hear the truth, because while people lie, their energy doesn't. It's easy to tell if an intimate partner is hiding something or if there are unresolved issues in a relationship that need to be addressed. You know this, you feel it, but you need validation. Or maybe you don't want validation—but the truth is an energetic form, and you can't mess with energy. Even Einstein made us aware of the many different levels of energy and that it cannot be created or destroyed. It can only transform. When I do readings, I am simply voicing something that my clients already know. Their intuition has picked up on something wrong and they're coming to me for confirmation. I give them the best description of what I am interpreting from the energy, but it is always up to the clients (or you, when you learn how to interpret your own energy) to use that information for their own best interest. Sadly, many people ignore the information because it's NOT what they want to hear. But Divine Love or the God Consciousness does not want us to suffer, and it is no accident that a person has come for guidance.

There are what I call "currents" of universal energy that enable us to sense whether we are going to meet someone special in the future. It's interesting that many of the individuals in our current lives have been part of our past lives as well—in different forms, perhaps, but still in relationship to us. Sometimes we get that déjà vu feeling when we meet someone, but we can never figure out what it is. Perhaps it is that the person is from a past life relationship and we are reconnecting to support each other or to reconcile some unfinished business or to complete a potential lesson that we are meant to learn. **However, it's very important to remember that while some things are predestined, our actions are not.** We may be destined to meet a potential partner, but the choices we make will determine whether we fall in love or pass the person by, or whether the relationship is more roses than thorns or vice versa.

Remember this: you have intuition that you can use to connect with loved ones, to make your relationships better, and to sense what the universe has in store for you.

Here is a simple exercise to help you get better connected to your inner voice:

Whenever you have a question or an opportunity comes up, take a few moments to consult your own inner wisdom. Preferably you'd be in a quiet place, alone and able to concentrate. But even if you are on a subway platform surrounded by people or waiting in line at the mall, imagine that a bright white light is radiating from your core as if you were the sun. Ask your question or say hello to your loved one, and then listen for a response. You'll be amazed at how much you already know or sense when you simply take the time to pay attention.

CHAPTER 2

But He's My Soul Mate!

(True or False?)

A lot of people today seem to be fixated on the idea of finding their soul mate. However, there is a mistaken idea of what a "soul mate" really is. So many books have been published on the subject of knowing who your soul mate is, attracting him or her, and creating a relationship. As a result, we all feel that we're looking for a cosmic, undying bond that transcends time and space, so we'll walk away from wonderful relationships if they don't shake us to our core the way we feel they should. Most people's views of soul mates are fantasies, like Romeo and Juliet or Cinderella and her Prince—and those fantasies can get in the way of finding and creating a lasting relationship with an intimate partner. It's also important to remember that a soul mate isn't just a romantic partner. Some of your best friends are your soul mates—it's the nature of the eternal connection of love.

As I mentioned, there have been volumes written on this topic by notable people such as Brian Weiss and Sandy Anastasi, and while all these experts may have some minor differences, we all agree on one thing: **A soul mate is someone who helps your soul to grow.**

Our spirits are part of a web of interconnected loving relationships that extends far beyond just one lifetime. It's as if the earth is a boarding school where we come back to attend classes year after year, life after life. At this school we have many familiar "classmates" who are learning their own lessons and making progress while helping us to do the same. Those classmates are our soul mates. Because of our love for one another, we agree to come back together and to help each other learn and grow. Through our many incarnations we develop many relationships. These relationships travel from one lifetime to another, yet you can have many soul mates that choose to take many different forms. Your soul mate could be your spouse, your parent, your child, your best friend, or your worst enemy. And let's not forget our furry friends: our pets! I've known people who have rescued a dog or cat say, "He picked us!" It could be that unconditional love you never had from a previous life's relationship and now the dog has come back to serve you! You could meet or be in relationship with your soul mates this time around, or you could never get to know them because they're off learning important lessons that don't involve you. As psychiatrist Brian Weiss puts it, you are eternally linked to your soul "classmates," but sometimes you may need to take separate classes.

We get into trouble when we start to believe that the only relationship worth having is with a soul mate. When the fireworks aren't immediate or the connection isn't instant, this belief makes us think that the relationship isn't worth our time.

The truth is that we have many soul mates that incarnate in many forms over many lifetimes, depending on the lessons we—and they—need to learn. This time around, take a look at your life so far to see which people have had the most impact on you. There's a good chance that they are your soul mates. **Remember, a soul mate is someone who brings more love and meaning into your life.** So take that off your list of "must haves" because you already have soul mates all around you. That is NOT to say a romantic love cannot be a soul mate—just don't limit your thinking!

The truth is that **we do not need anyone else to be complete and whole.** If we continually are looking outside ourselves for something or someone to fill us up or to make us feel loved, we are setting ourselves up for a lifetime of hurt and a feeling of emptiness.

Many myths have been built around soul mates, which can actually stop us from finding the love that we are searching for. Here are five primary myths about soul mates that I've heard or read about. How many of these myths have you believed in over the years? Learning the truth can help you in your quest to find and sustain a great intimate relationship.

MYTH 1: Your soul mate is your perfect relationship, your "other half" who makes you feel complete.

Instead of looking *outside* for love, we need to look *within*, at the love that is our nature. Each one of us is a spark of divine love that has chosen to come to earth. We are love. We are made of love—love lies at our core. The great spiritual traditions of the world teach us that all we need to do is recognize the love we have within. After that, we can access it and feel it at any moment. When my father would kiss me goodnight, he would always say: "Say your prayers: 'God is love, love is God, you are loved, and we love you.'"

When we recognize our own loving, divine heart, we do not need anyone else's love to feel complete and whole. I know that's a very hard concept to wrap our brain—and our hearts—around, but it is true. Whatever your religious background is, you have been taught that God Loves You. Unfortunately, when we feel unloved by others, we forget or ignore that very simple fact. So we choose to create relationships here on earth to give and receive love, and too often we become more identified with the relationships rather than the love-based energy we all possess. And it is that essence of love that we want to share with others and have them share with us—because when we share that love with others, we feel wonderful. The great psychic Edgar Cayce said that we're attracted to a soul mate because by being with that person we are inspired to become whole ourselves. But remember it is only the *inspiration* we long for, because we were born complete. We just need to recognize the beauty of our own souls and share it with others.

MYTH 2: You have just one soul mate who keeps reincarnating as your lover.

I read a story recently about a woman who married a much older man, and they both were very happy—except every now and then, without thinking, she would call him "Dad." As you can imagine, this was pretty upsetting to them both. They went to see a psychic, who told them that the woman had been the man's daughter in a previous lifetime, but that she had died very young. "You still had lessons to learn from each other," the psychic said, "so you were drawn together in a different relationship this time around." The truth is that our soul mates take many different forms from lifetime to lifetime, depending on the lessons we need to learn. Like this woman, one of your soul mates can be your father in one life, your husband in another, your child or best friend in a third. It's also possible that your intimate partner is a new soul, a new energy drawn to you for your mutual benefit. But never think that there's only "one" perfect match for you in earth or in heaven. Again, remember that soul mates come in many shapes and sizes: when it comes to lifetimes, your soul mate is not one-size-fits-all! There's far too much love in the universe for there to be only one channel through which it can flow.

MYTH 3: You know your soul mates instantly because you feel a deep connection to them.

When you feel that tingle or those butterflies in the stomach, it's not necessarily your soul connecting to another soul. It could be as simple as "chemistry" (see page 94 for an in-depth discussion of the differences between soul mate chemistry and sexual chemistry). Until then, it's important to be careful in assuming that (1) someone is your soul mate when you feel an instant connection, or (2) someone isn't your soul mate because you don't. Of course, there are people with whom you can feel connected the moment you meet. It could be a previous life experience making its presence known, but your destiny could be to learn to recognize love in other forms. What if the lesson your soul needs this time around is to learn to love someone gradually, over time? Or what if the connection you feel is simply biochemistry? Don't worry; we'll get to that puzzlement a little later.

It's also possible that the connection you feel comes from three other sources:

• This person may remind you of a past incarnation. Perhaps you meet a tall, beautiful man from Ireland and are instantly attracted to him, but you don't know why. Maybe you're unconsciously remembering a past life in Ireland, and just the sound of his accent was enough to feel a connection with this person.

• You may feel a connection to someone that is what I call a "karmic" relationship. You may have some unfinished karma with this person from a prior lifetime. For example, imagine that in your last lifetime you were a heartbreaker, loving and leaving behind a string of people in the egotistic pursuit of your own desires. All the people you hurt were not necessarily soul mates, but your actions caused you to accrue some pretty negative romantic karma. Your lesson this time around might be for you to be the one to love and be left repeatedly. You may feel a deep connection with this person in the moment because her task in this lifetime is to dump you once she gains your heart.

• You may feel an instant connection that may have nothing to do with karma, or finding your soul mate, or even past lives—instead, you may simply have an immense amount in common with this person. It could be that this is the **first** relationship you will have for many lifetimes to come!

A Note on Karma

When we accrue karma in one lifetime, it's like we've amassed a cosmic debt that needs to be repaid before we can move on. Once the debt is finished, we become free and clear to learn, grow, and love in new relationships. I saw this happen with a friend of a friend who was married for twenty years and then, out of the blue, left his wife for another woman. He said it was as if his karma was done in his first relationship and they were both free to move on. Today he and his ex-wife are happily married to new partners. If you've ever been in a relationship for weeks, months, or years and then felt a sense of completion with this person, you know what it's like when your karma with someone is done. Yet these karmic relationships can often be very intense while they last.

In Chapter 10 we'll discuss how to use skills like intuition, astrology, and numerology to determine the kind of connection you and a potential lover possess.

Ultimately, looking for a soul mate connection can keep you from recognizing all the potential partners out there. Sometimes searching for "Mr. Perfect" keeps us from finding "Mr. Right." And face it: nobody's perfect!

Love is all around us; it shows up in many forms and grows at different speeds. If you're waiting for a soul mate and shutting out other love until you feel instant sparks, you may end up in a very lonely place. Love and companionship happen on many different levels, and ignoring everything but what you feel is a true soul mate connection will lead you to miss out on other important relationships.

MYTH 4: If you don't find your soul mate this time around, you're doomed to a life of lesser relationships, or no relationship at all.

Don't panic! It IS possible to have a great relationship with someone who isn't a soul mate. We can create great relationships with souls who wish the best for us, just as we do for them.

Souls come into this world at different levels. Some are old souls who have incarnated many times before, and there are younger souls. It's parallel to our own interpretation of young and old. An old soul has accumulated a certain wisdom that may seem unusual. You've heard the expression "wiser than her years." That doesn't mean people won't behave like party animals, but there is a noticeable difference in those who have a greater sense of spiritual, emotional, and physical balance. That "old soul" may choose to enter into a relationship in order to help a younger soul on life's journey. So the people we attract or to whom we are attracted may be new to us, but through our mutual love we can grow together for this lifetime, and perhaps for every lifetime after this one.

Love and growth are our two primary purposes here on earth, and when we open our hearts to an intimate partner, we can attract compatible energies that have goals that resonate with us.

MYTH 5: **Your soul mate is predestined.**

When people utter this myth of never finding their soul mate, it's possible they are using it as an excuse (1) to stay in an unfulfilling relationship that they know they should leave, (2) not to do the work to make their current relationship better, or (3) to avoid having to seek out a relationship at all. Let's face it: relationships aren't easy. But they can be immensely rewarding, and we need them to progress in this life and our subsequent lives.

You are probably wondering if there are some relationships that we are predestined to enter into. Of course. There is the ongoing debate of "free will vs. predestination." I believe both are at play: you're born with a map (predestination means the roads, highways, paths, mountains, rivers, and oceans are already in place), but how you get to your destination is your free will. But while predestination plays a part in the path of our lives, free will and choice play an even larger role. If there's a big sign that says DANGER–DETOUR and you chose to ignore it, that is free will. To use a familiar metaphor, each incarnation is like a hand of cards: we receive a certain number of cards when we're born, but how we play them is up to us. Life and relationships are what you (and your partner) make them. You just have to play the hand you're dealt to the best of your ability.

MYTH 6: **Once you find your soul mate, your relationship will be perfect.**

Wishing for a soul mate can be dangerous, because you never know what lessons your soul mate has to teach you, and to learn himself. I wish I could tell you that when and if you find your soul mate your relationship will be one of incredible love and closeness for years, but I can't.

A soul mate is someone who helps your soul to grow—and it's very possible that your soul mate came to earth this time to push all of your buttons! What if the lessons you need to learn in your relationships are patience, kindness, forgiveness, and tolerance? Or maybe your lesson this time is to stand up for yourself and have the courage to leave.

Our relationships, like our lives on earth, are designed as places where we grow. That's their main function in our soul's development. And if we have issues to work out, they have to be resolved before we can progress to higher levels on this earthly plane and on the other side as well. It's better to face the music now and get into step. Otherwise we'll just have to come back and work on these lessons again and again in future lifetimes.

Here are what I believe to be some of the key truths about soul mates:

- Every soul exists to love and be loved.

- Our nature is love, and that's why we crave relationships: to be able to express our nature and to grow in love and goodness by learning about ourselves and others.

- We each have many "soul mates," defined as other souls who are committed to help us learn and grow, both here and on the other side.

- These soul mates can incarnate as our parents, siblings, children, friends, lovers, and enemies. We will encounter soul mates depending on the lessons we most need to learn.

- Some of our relationships are predestined—we are meant to meet certain people, for example, and perhaps fall in love or be in conflict with them—but we are responsible for the choices we make in those relationships.

- All our intimate relationships are not necessarily with our soul mates, but that doesn't make them less passionate or valuable. There can be more than one Mr. or Ms. Right out there for each of us, because our souls need different things to grow at different times.

- Don't put your life on hold waiting for your soul mate to show up. It's far more important to learn to give and receive love from the people you meet. That way, if your soul mate does appear, you'll be ready. And if your soul mate isn't a lover this time around, you won't have shut yourself off from the love the universe wants you to share.

- Ultimately, the purpose of our soul mates and of our relationships in general—indeed, the purpose of our incarnating—is to learn and grow in love, wisdom, and goodness, so that we may become more like God.

Most importantly, realize that every soul has the chance for love. We are born from love, into love, and our purpose on earth is to better learn how to give and receive love.

There will always be bumps in the road while we work through the good times and bad, let go if necessary, and learn the lessons that will help us grow.

CHAPTER 3

Lights! Camera! Action!

Getting Ready for Your "Close-Up"

Face it: you wouldn't go to a special party wearing something shabby. You want to look your best. It's important to put your best foot forward, so why not your best inner spirit? Remember the phrase "it's beauty from within"? It's true! You need to radiate the brightest, most beautiful part of your soul. But before we get into the inner beauty makeover, I want to talk a little about opposites: do they really attract?

You've heard it many times: when it comes to love, opposites attract. Most of us have had that experience at least once in our lives. However, I have found that more often we don't attract our opposite; in fact, I believe that we attract partners who are our energetic match. Either their energy is similar to ours, or it complements some aspect of our makeup. If you've ever seen the movie *Grease*, you've see this principle in action. Sweet Sandy brings out the sincere, loving heart of biker Danny, and Danny brings out the wild side in her. If, as we said in the last chapter, the purpose of our relationships is to help our souls grow in learning and love, then it makes sense that **the partners we draw to us are reflections of our energy and the state of our soul development.** That's why, as Edgar Cayce remarked, it's extremely important for us to make sure our energy is healthy, balanced, and clear, so that we can draw the best relationship to us and keep that relationship healthy through time.

Let's start with my mantra for anyone wanting to get into a great relationship: first we must *get whole, get clear, and get bal-*

Those whose
SUFFERING
is due to
LOVE
are, as we say
of certain invalids,
their own physicians.

MARCEL PROUST

anced. Call it an assessment of our personal and spiritual wardrobe. These three words represent different aspects of preparing ourselves to attract and keep the best partners for us. These people will fill our hearts and make our souls happy, and we can do the same for them. But we must start with self-love. I don't mean an ego-driven love. Self-love is something within ourselves that radiates out into the world. Think of it as a light beam. The brighter it shines, the more illuminated everything becomes! We must be complete in ourselves before we can give freely and fully to another person. Too often we look for others to fill in the gaps we feel in ourselves, which is not only unfair to them, but to ourselves as well. When we depend on the people around us to make ourselves whole, we miss out on an important part of our own growth. We must understand our reasons for seeking a relationship, to make sure there are no ulterior motives or desires. We must make sure we are balanced emotionally and psychologically, removing any past blocks that might get in the way of our loving and being loved. Only then are we ready to prepare ourselves to seek the love that will fulfill us at the highest level.

GET WHOLE: *You Are Totally Complete Just As You Are*

Have you ever been around someone who was either needy or desperate? How attractive did you find that person's energy? So why is it that we don't recognize neediness when we go out searching for an intimate relationship? The worst energy we can project is that we somehow "need" a relationship. Using the wardrobe analogy, remember—you are not naked. When you are whole, you are fully clothed in your most radiant attire. But if you are needy and desperate, it's like wearing something frumpy— that energy drives people away instead of pulling them in.

Unfortunately, far too many of us confuse love and need when it comes to relationships. If someone needs us, we think, *Great—I'll be there for this person and they'll be there for me.* But if you've ever been in a relationship with someone who "needed" you, maybe just a little too much, you probably recognized that the need created an unhealthy dependence, perhaps even a feeling of smothering. And if you are the one who expresses need, you probably feel as if you are begging for crumbs...which makes you feel crummier! A healthy, whole partner will be attracted to another healthy person (unless they're not *truly* healthy—but more on that later). True intimacy is the result of completeness joining completeness, when we bring our wholeness to a relationship with another complete human being. We know that we are ready for a heavenly relationship only when we feel we are whole and complete in ourselves, with or without a partner. We need to feel good about ourselves and appreciate our own best qualities, which are what we bring to a relationship. Going back to the wardrobe analogy: you find your prettiest dress, you do your hair and makeup—would you expect to wear your boyfriend's shoes to complete your outfit? Of course not. You need to have your own spiritual wardrobe complete.

All love begins with the knowledge that we are divine and made of love and therefore worthy of love shared with someone else. When we feel this love, it's easy for us to give love freely and openly. We will also attract someone with the same level of love inside. When I say "feel the love," I don't mean that we should receive it from an external force. On the contrary: our connection with the divine comes from within.

If you are coming out of a bad relationship (or you are in one currently), it can be very difficult to recognize and acknowledge your wholeness and unique gifts. It may seem difficult—almost impossible—but you can and must find reasons to love yourself. We can have that "heavenly" feeling only when we truly feel connected to the divine. And that's when we can create heavenly love in our lives. When we feel whole, we recognize other souls who are whole in themselves. When we feel whole, others treat us as whole and complete. Your love and self-worth come from inside yourself, from your very nature. They radiate from within.

The best part is that when we are whole and complete in ourselves, we can be happy whether we're in a relationship or not. We can be alone and still feel loved. When we know ourselves, we are less likely to fall for someone's outward appearance or our childhood dreams of the perfect partner, and we are more likely to be attracted to someone who resonates with our deepest, truest impulses.

Now you might ask, "I do feel whole and complete, so why do I keep attracting the same kind of partner?" As I mentioned earlier, we often need to have certain experiences to learn certain lessons in order to progress to the next level in our soul's journey. But I can promise you, if you are aware and complete, if you enter a relationship that doesn't support you for the long term, you will figure it out more quickly if you love yourself. Our wake-up call often comes when we start to notice that we're no longer "ourselves." We may notice that we're trying to be something or someone we're not in order to satisfy our partners. In heavenly relationships, we become more like ourselves, not less. We should feel free to be honest, to express ourselves openly, and to ask the same of our partner.

When we are complete and whole, we recognize that the experience of love does not come from someone else but arises from deep within ourselves. As spiritual teacher Byron Katie says, it's as if your beloved has held up a mirror and showed you your own heart. We don't "lose" ourselves in our relationship; we simply discover deeper and deeper levels of love within as well as without.

Shakespeare described love as "boundless as the sea": infinite, never-ending, emanating from the one true divine source of all love. When we know the source of love is inside us rather than outside in another, then we will bring our whole selves into the relationship. And when two whole people join, their love creates something far greater than just two halves coming together. They become a model of love for the world.

GET CLEAR: *What Are Your Reasons for Being in a Relationship?*

To prepare yourself for the great relationship you desire and deserve, you need to examine your reasons for wanting to be in one. As you learned in the last chapter, the purpose of our relationships here on earth is so we can learn how to give and receive love at ever greater levels. When we enter a relationship for the wrong reasons, it also can lead to growth—but often of the painful kind.

I'm sure you've known people who married their partners for money, or security, or status, or sexual attraction. Unfortunately, most of those relationships do not end well, unless there is true, unselfish love between partners. Think about it. If your primary reason for getting into a relationship is financial, or because your partner gives you stability and security, or simply because you think your sweetie is hot, what happens if those conditions change, as they almost invariably do? I've found that people who marry for money pay for it the rest of their lives. Often they find themselves in an inferior position in the relationship. They're afraid to leave because it would mean a lower standard of living, and as a result they put up with a lot more than they should.

For a relationship to be successful for the long term, both partners need to feel they are bringing value into the partnership. It doesn't mean that you should only date people who are your financial equal or that you can only be attracted to someone who is your equal in looks. But it does mean that you need to have a clear sense of your own self-worth. You need to enter into the relationship not for what the other person owns or makes or looks like, but because of who she is. Think about relationships in which one partner falls ill, or loses his job and income, or changes physically due to old age, and the other partner still loves him regardless. Such relationships are often an inspiration to the rest of us.

In preparing yourself for a true, deep, intimate relationship, you need to start by examining your own reasons for wanting one, and make sure there are no ulterior motives.

Tick-tock: Unfortunately, one ulterior motive that I see very frequently among women, anywhere from their twenties to their forties, is the desire to have a child. As women start moving into their thirties they feel their biological clocks ticking, and they desperately start to search for a partner to marry and start a family. They'll turn a blind eye to obvious flaws in a partner simply because they're worried about waiting too long to have children. But while it's natural to want a family, it shouldn't be your only reason for seeking a relationship. What if you can't have children or your partner doesn't want them? Would you want to be in a relationship with someone who regards you simply as a means to an end? This is one area in which I believe you should let destiny play itself out. If you are meant to have kids, you'll have them. If there is a child waiting on the other side for you to be its parent, then you will be that child's parent, whether you're in a relationship or you decide to have a child without a partner. But choosing a mate only because you need someone to father your child is not a recipe for a great relationship, and it probably won't provide the best environment for any child, either. These are often the relationships that end as soon as the last child leaves home. You deserve a better relationship than that. Take the time to find a partner you can love for himself, not just because of the possibility of children.

Fixer-upper: Another very bad reason to get into a relationship is to "fix" a partner. This is a trap that many people in the helping professions, like nurses, physicians, and therapists, fall into. People who have worked hard to make sure they are healthy and whole sometimes feel that they need to rescue someone who is hurting. They apply the same impulses they use in their professional lives—being a healer, caring for the sick and wounded—to their relationships. But to have a healthy, heavenly relationship, you need to differentiate between lovers and patients. You cannot fix anyone. I repeat: you cannot fix anyone. People can only fix themselves. Whenever a healthy partner tries to fix an unhealthy one, all it does is breed either dependency or resentment—or both. You absolutely deserve a healthy relationship with another healthy soul. That's who you need to look for. If you are looking for someone to fix, then you're probably not as healthy and whole as you thought. (See the warning on being "needed" earlier in this chapter.) Trying to fix someone who is broken will only leave you with broken dreams and the inevitable, downward spiral of your self-worth.

Don't be a scaredy-cat! One of the other bad reasons for getting into a relationship—or staying out of one—is fear. I'm sure you've seen people who are afraid of being alone and will take up with almost anyone to prevent that from happening. Or perhaps they've had some bad experiences and they're afraid of *getting* into a relationship because they don't want to get hurt again. Fear can stop you from expressing your true desires and acting on them. Fear of being alone is one of the worst reasons for getting into a relationship, and of course, staying away from relationships out of fear and hurt means you will miss out on some of the most important aspects of life here on earth.

Need to please: The approval or disapproval of those we care about also can be very powerful reasons for wanting a relationship. How important is it to you that your family and friends approve of your choice of partner? How would you feel if your lover was not acceptable to them for reasons of ethnicity, age, sex, financial status, and so on? Certainly we want to pay attention to our friends and family because they have our best interests at heart. They often see things in our potential partners that we may not be able to see. However, if you choose a partner based on the approval of your friends and family, you are setting yourself up for a lot of potential pain.

Seeking outside approval usually means that you are not strong enough emotionally to know what you want and to ask for it. You are seeking outside validation rather than inner confirmation of your choice, and anytime you rate "outside" love as a higher priority than your own inner love, you are doomed to disappointment. The only place where you should look for approval is inside yourself, where you will find your inner wisdom—your own personal connection to the loving energy of the universe.

※※※※※※※

You also need to be clear about your expectations and standards: what do you expect from a partner? If your choice of mate is in alignment with what the universe wants for you, then it should not matter whether or not your friends and family approve.

Seek approval from your inner knowing. Base your choices on your ability to love yourself and others freely, and you will be approaching relationships from the best possible perspective.

I will caution you, however, that friends and family may see things you don't see about the person. It happened to me. In one recent relationship I was so "in love with love" that I was blind to certain unhealthy behavior in my partner. My friends and family helped tip me off so I could see the truth. Then I was able to act in my own best interests and leave the relationship. But had I not had a sense of self, self-love, and understood and appreciated divine love, I would most likely still be in a very bad situation, wondering how I missed that bus coming straight at me!

So take a few minutes to think about all the reasons you want to get into a relationship. Yes, relationships take work. They are inevitably both exciting and painful. You need to be willing to commit a lot of time, energy, and emotion to them. Why do you want a relationship in your life right now? Be honest with yourself. If you find a reason that's less than positive—financial security, a way to avoid loneliness, your biological clock, a need for approval, and so on—it's a sign that you may need to do some inner work to get balanced. That's not bad, but it is important to know before you start to look for love.

GET BALANCED: *Take Care of Any Blocks to a Healthy Relationship*

Have you ever felt just a little "off" physically, not sick but not completely well either? Often that feeling of being "off" is either a precursor to a real illness or a signal that there's something wrong on a deeper level. The same thing is true of our emotional and psychological health. If we're feeling a little "off" emotionally or psychologically, it could be that we are simply in a funk or working through a particular problem, but it could also be a signal that an unacknowledged issue is brewing just below the surface. We must be aware if there is anything that is blocking our energy and preventing us from feeling healthy and balanced. The only time we are able to create healthy relationships is when we are healthy ourselves.

When I teach people to develop their intuition, I talk a lot about the importance of balance. Any kind of energy blockage can prevent you from tuning in to the subtle messages from the universe. The same is true when it comes to our relationships.

The only way we will attract great partners is if our energy is clear, balanced, and expressive of our wholeness and self-love. However, many people have energy blocks keeping them from successful relationships. These blocks are often self-inflicted. They can be caused by past relationships with parents, siblings, lovers, or even relationships from previous lifetimes. If we don't get rid of these blocks, we end up playing out the same dysfunctional relationship patterns again and again. They can also prevent us from seeing the very partners that would be absolutely perfect for us. That's why it's so important to identify and heal any emotional or psychological blocks that are standing in the way of your heavenly relationship. Remember, thoughts are energy, and every energy has its own density. Perhaps that's why it's called a block: a high-density energy that is holding you back from moving forward. If you have a block, then that energy needs to be shifted.

CHAPTER 4

The Keys to Your Karmic Love Commandments

"Know thyself" is one of the most important commandments we can follow when it comes to loving and being loved. I believe there are many keys to making sure you are healthy and balanced emotionally and psychologically. Here are a few important truths—I'll call them the Karmic Love Commandments—you will need to understand in order to create a successful relationship. If you find yourself struggling with one of these issues, this may be a signal that you need help clearing the energy blocks that may have created the problem.

You Must Never Feel You Have to Pretend You're Something You're Not in Order to Be in a RELATIONSHIP

Long ago there was a wonderful play in which each character held a mask in front of his or her face. They would speak one set of lines through the mask, and then they would turn to the audience and say what was really going on in their minds. Unfortunately, that's how many of us approach relationships. We have a mask, a persona, that we show the people we are dating (or even living with), because we think it's what they want, but underneath is our true self, who we really are. And our partners have done the exact same thing. On top of that, each of us has created an image of the perfect partner, and that's what we are looking for. That's often what we fall in love with. So we hide behind our mask while looking for another mask, never really finding the partner we want because we can't see the truth behind the facade. The relationship we end up with is just two masks looking at each other, creating a fake relationship based on illusions, lies, and fear. For instance, in one long-distance relationship a man told a friend of mine that he would move wherever she was living so they could be together. Months later he confessed that he had only said that because he thought it was what she wanted to hear. Is it any wonder that the real people behind the masks are often angry, unhappy, upset, or just plain unfulfilled?

If we don't allow ourselves to be ourselves in relationship, if we feel we have to hide behind a mask, it's because of an unspoken fear: "You won't love me as I am and I won't love you as you are." This kind of behavior arises from a lack of self-love. How many of us have said some version of the old refrain, "I hate my (fill in the blank: nose, arms, legs, skin)?" Or we've been on a date or putting up a profile on the Internet and lied about our economic status, our job, or where we live just because we didn't feel that the truth was good enough? You make an assumption that a potential partner will not love you for the same reason that you don't love yourself. Although it's true that some people have certain expectations (looks, age, income), you really don't want to be with someone who has a checklist that you must try to aspire to. That's their issue. You have your own checklist: someone who will love YOU for who YOU are—not your age, income, or zip code.

Spiritual teacher Don Miguel Ruiz wrote that everyone has a price that is measured in self-love. We set that price, and life respects it. In terms of love and respect from others, we will get from life the price that we ask. In other words, the amount of love and respect we receive is based on the amount of love and respect we have for ourselves. That is a very profound lesson to learn when it comes to our emotional health and balance. We must be willing to love ourselves, to be ourselves, and to ask for the same love and respect that we would give to others. That's the balanced and healthy way to enter a relationship.

Be Willing to Face the TRUTH

The only way to ensure that you are psychologically and emotionally healthy is to be willing to face the truth about yourself and your blocks. This means you have to stop denying your problems and issues and be honest with yourself. So many people go for readings and counseling, but they're not looking for truth—they just want confirmation of the lies they're telling about themselves and their relationships.

As all the twelve-step and other addiction recovery programs will tell you, the first step to health is to admit you have a problem. That means you have to be honest about yourself, your needs, your blocks, and your good and bad experiences with relationships. It also means being honest about your good points as well. (See previous discussions on self-worth on page 25 and page 35.) You need to have the courage to be completely honest with yourself. Believe me, I know this is not easy! But when you are honest with yourself, you will have a clearer picture of what's great about you and what you need work on. You'll have a road map to follow that will help you on your path to a heavenly relationship. And if you continue to check in with yourself to make sure you are being true to your inner wisdom, this will also keep you on the path by reminding you to be honest with yourself and your partner.

Be Willing to Be VULNERABLE

The only way to create a great relationship is to be brave enough to be vulnerable. If we have been hurt in previous relationships—and very few of us haven't been hurt in love at some point—this can be one of our biggest barriers to loving and being loved. Any barriers we put around our heart to keep people out also keep us trapped in our own insecurities. They stop us from giving our love freely. And while they may protect us, they confine us even more, keeping us from pursuing the love that we want to give and receive.

Many people have trouble with vulnerability because they associate it with weakness. But in truth, the only way to let love into our lives is to be vulnerable. In the long run, a lack of openness and vulnerability will kill a relationship. If you do not let your partner in, if you're not willing to reveal your pain as well as your strengths, if you have to be in control or in charge all the time, how can you expect your partner to feel close to you? Our strengths may make us admirable, but our weakness and openness make us approachable. If you are afraid to be vulnerable because of old wounds or because you think that vulnerability is weak and you must be strong, you have emotional and psychological work to do before you can get into a great relationship.

Never Love BLINDLY *or Feel That Love Must Be Unconditional*

It may seem strange to you to read that loving blindly or unconditionally can be a threat to balance, but these two illusions about love can cause considerable pain and injury. By definition, if you love blindly, you're not seeing the reality of the other person: as I have discussed, you've probably fallen in love with your image of a lover instead of who this person really is on the inside. Blind love rarely lasts, because eventually we have to open our eyes to what's really there. In contrast, real love allows us to see the other completely, fully, "warts and all," recognizing both strengths and weaknesses.

I'm also very leery of anyone who tells me that love should be "unconditional." You may be familiar with some famous cases of "unconditional love" between a partner who committed a serious crime and his beloved, who knew about it and let him get away with it because of love despite all obstacles. And what about people whose partners cheat on them repeatedly and yet they keep taking the philanderers back? That is not "unconditional" love—that's being a doormat. It does nothing to help either partner learn and grow; in fact, all it does is condone negative patterns of behavior.

Love *should* have conditions—the main condition being that both partners are committed to loving and growing together. If one partner has rules and boundaries that the other knowingly violates, there need to be consequences; otherwise, eventually there will be a loss of respect on one side, loss of self-esteem on the other, and a loss of love for both.

A heavenly relationship needs to abide by the laws of heaven, which include mutual trust, respect, and regard. When those three things are present, love can grow in the way that it is meant to: inside each partner and between them both.

CHAPTER 5

If Your Spirit Has a Boo-Boo:

Healing Yourself and Your Ability to Love

How do you know that you need healing? Sometimes it's pretty clear: if the word "relationship" makes you turn and run, or if all your memories of a romantic partner are painful, or if you simply have given up finding an intimate relationship. If any of that sounds familiar, you probably know you have some inner work to do before you find a great partner.

However, sometimes the psychological or emotional clues are subtler. What are your beliefs when it comes to relationships? If someone asks you about romance or finding a partner, do you find yourself saying things like "All the good ones are taken" or "I'm too busy for a relationship" or "I have to put my kids first right now" or "It's just not worth the hassle"?

These beliefs, even if they're expressed casually or in fun, indicate that you have bad associations with relationships, which may get in the way of finding a partner and creating a great relationship.

The good news is that sometimes all it takes to shift these ideas is to get some distance from these issues. Have you ever had a bad breakup with someone and afterward sworn you would never fall in love again? After a certain amount of time you find that the pain has faded, and you become open to the idea of a new partner and meeting new people. Even better news is that there are ways to accelerate this process of recovery, allowing you to deal more quickly with beliefs that have become entrenched in your psyche.

I'm a big advocate of getting professional help anytime you have unresolved issues of any kind, especially if you have had challenges with relationships. My sister Alicia is a psychologist who also works on relationship issues. Although her clinical training is based in science and mine is based on an intuitive knowledge of the human spirit, we both believe in the concept of seeking help to accelerate healing. Through our work we have found that if there are barriers preventing you from being in a romantic relationship, you should take a look at the following three areas to see if you need to work on them, either by yourself or with the help of a professional:

Your Relationship with Your PARENTS

Scientists have described something called "attachment disorder," which means that people who are not cared for and loved in childhood have trouble forming long-term relationships. Essentially, they don't have enough experience of love and nurturing when they're young and so their brains don't learn how to connect with others at that level. Luckily, most of us have had at least one loving adult in our lives, whether it be a parent, stepparent, grandparent, aunt, uncle, even an older brother, sister, or cousin. No one is born a "professional parent": everyone begins the parenting process as an amateur. Too often our parents pass along their own limitations and insecurities about love. Consequently we duplicate those feelings when it comes to our own relationships.

Were your parents openly affectionate with each other? Chances are, that's what you crave in your own partner. Were your folks critical or prone to complaining, never satisfied with you or each other or anyone else? Their style of relating will affect what you expect in a relationship, and, unless you are self-aware, you will most likely follow suit. Children who were raised by critical parents can become people-pleasers, always looking to get the approval of their partners. Unfortunately, they often attract supercritical people into their lives, thus duplicating their parents' patterns. Or if they were raised in an abusive or alcoholic family, they can seek out partners with the same patterns and try to "fix" them. Their partners become surrogates for the families that the children were never able to heal.

As a psychotherapist who does a lot of family counseling, Alicia can attest to the influence of our parents when it comes to our ability to relate to others: "Children learn what they live. Parents are a child's most powerful role model! When we are blessed, as my sisters and I were, to be brought up by parents who treated each other, us, and others with love, kindness, and respect, we learn to do the same." That's why it's so important to be clear about the patterns we pick up from our parents—to take the best from their relationship and leave the rest behind. I've often observed that people seem to be drawn to partners who are like the parent from whom they wanted love but who didn't reciprocate. Most of us wanted the love of one parent more than the other, usually from the one who didn't provide as much affection. This is a very normal psychological response, yet it can play out destructively when we seek the same missing affection in our adult intimate relationships. It is common for men to fall in love with women who are like their mothers, or women with men like their fathers. But if the parent whose love you craved was abusive or distant, or had addiction issues, it is quite possible you will then unconsciously try to replicate those negative relationships.

If you feel you need help identifying and healing your relationship with your parents, find a good counselor and get to work. If you suspect that you simply had "amateur" parents who perhaps didn't do as well as they could have in being the best role models for a loving couple, you may find it helpful to first take a look at the relationship patterns you may have adopted in your childhood. Our parents shape our earliest ideas of relationships, so it's useful to write down what we think our parents may have thought about this important topic. Your ideas may be true or false, but the main thing is that you believe them to be accurate.

LET'S GET BUSY

Grab your journal—or something that will serve as your journal from now on.

Begin by writing down everything you remember about your parents' relationship. It doesn't have to be a complete narrative— just a few words or sentences of your best recollections.

1. Were they affectionate? Busy? Harsh? Distant? Loving? Fun-loving?

2. Describe their relationship with each other, the good and the bad. If your parents divorced and remarried while you were young, describe the relationship you remember the best or you believe had the most impact.

3. If someone other than your parents raised you, describe your primary caregivers and their relationships.

4. Describe your relationship with your parents—separately, then together (or if you were part of a blended family, your relationship with the adults who had the most presence in your life).

   • Were they disciplinarians? Casual? Happy? Critical?

   • Did they have high or low standards?

   • What made them happy or angry about you?

   • How did they relate to you, and did they relate in different ways to your siblings?

   • Which parent's love did you crave the most?

5. Now, write down a description of what you believe your parents believed about relationships and love.

Once you have written all this down, read it over and see if you can spot any ideas, beliefs, or experiences that are shaping your ability to be in an intimate relationship.

Often just realizing where your blocks may be coming from can be of enormous help in getting rid of them. If, for example, you had a dad who was fun-loving but irresponsible, and as an adult you find yourself in relationship after relationship with guys whose motto seems to be "Party, love 'em, and leave 'em," you can understand where your attraction to such men comes from. After you become aware of this pattern, you'll be able to begin looking for someone who is fun-loving yet reliable and interested in long-term relationships.

One of the biggest steps we can take in healing relationships with our parents is to make peace with them. Forgive them for being amateurs. No one is a perfect parent. Every one of us will mess things up in one way or another, even if we have the best intentions.

Here is another exercise to help heal issues you may have:

Close your eyes and envision your parents standing before you—whether they are here or have passed over. Tell them:

> *I forgive you for being amateurs.*
>
> *I forgive you for being human and making mistakes.*
>
> *I know you were doing the best you could.*
>
> *I ask you to forgive me for the times I wasn't loving to you.*
>
> *I appreciate the love you gave me, and I love you.*

Offer them the gift of your love and forgiveness. Maybe this is difficult, especially if this exercise brought up a lot of emotions, but once you start releasing lingering negative feelings, you will make room for more positive energies.

BUT—! One caveat about asking for and giving forgiveness: if there was a serious issue in your childhood with your parents—abuse, addiction, early death of mother or father, or anything that caused you serious pain that is still unresolved—please do not attempt this process unless you have gotten some kind of counseling to heal these complex psychological and emotional issues.

It is also important to remember that forgiveness doesn't mean forgetting if you have suffered harm from someone. You can forgive a parent who did not treat you well, but you can remember the lessons you learned from that treatment and resolve never to treat others the same way. Make sure you stay away from the residue of any negative energy caused by your relationship with your parents, so you can enter into your own romantic relationship free, clear, and happy.

Someone once said that our lives can be either examples or warnings to others. Both are beneficial.

Your PAST *Romantic Relationships*

If you've ever had a bad relationship, you know how important it is to heal yourself after it has ended. When you've been hurt in love, you feel raw. You simply can't imagine ever trusting anyone enough to open your heart ever again. And while most of us are eventually willing to get into another relationship, if something reminds us of the past, we can overreact, become extremely emotional, and even head for the door, because on a subconscious level we are expecting the same thing to happen to us again.

I did a reading for a gentleman whose first wife had cheated on him. Then his girlfriend did the same! He's moved on and is now happily married to his second wife, but he told me that he was still at a high level of anxiety all the time, just waiting for the moment when he finds out that she has cheated on him as well. His new wife probably has no intention of having an affair, but if he thinks *Are you cheating on me yet?* every time he sees her, what do you think is in store for that marriage? You guessed it: trouble!

We need to make sure there is no emotional unfinished business lingering from past relationships. Again, this is where some kind of therapy or counseling can be extremely useful, especially if a past affair left us feeling debilitated for a long time. Many of us can eventually process and get rid of these old negative associations on our own, but if they are truly paralyzing us with fear and doubt, counseling can help. And we all want to be ready for love sooner rather than later.

One of the ways you can pinpoint a lingering relationship issue is if you find yourself repeating patterns in consecutive relationships. For example, you leave one relationship because your partner is hypercritical and vow that in your next relationship you'll find someone who loves you no matter what. In your next relationship, you think that's who you've found, only to discover that while your new partner may say she loves you completely and without reservations, she makes little niggling comments that still let you know that she's criticizing you. You've unconsciously traded overt criticism for covert criticism, and it feels just as bad as it did the first time around.

You need to do some inner work to discover what is either causing you to choose critical partners or compelling you to read their comments as criticism. Regarding the latter option, this is not to say that your partner is in the right and that you're *not* being criticized. But do ask yourself if this is really the same problem you had in your first relationship. Have you inadvertently chosen an overly critical partner, or did problems in your first relationship cause you to become particularly sensitive to criticism? Remember, **the only one you can change in your relationship is yourself.** You're responsible for your half of the relationship, just as your partner is responsible for the other half. You take care of your half and then you can see if this relationship is really what you want.

When you clear the emotional blocks that came from past relationships, you'll feel lighter and freer and more open to love. You can still benefit from the lessons you learned—but you don't have to repeat the same mistakes. The good thing about freeing yourself from the negative associations of past relationships is that you're no longer hooked by old problems. You have emotionally rehabilitated and liberated yourself. Have you ever run into an ex-partner years after a relationship, when you think you're over it, and you see this person walking into the room with a new honey and you feel absolutely nothing? That's the point you want to get to with all your old relationships. You are over it!

Here's a suggestion for discovering any old relationships that still have power over you.

- Write down the name of every person you've had a romantic relationship with (if you can remember them all!) from your first crush to your current relationship, if you are in one.

- When you write the names, notice if there is any kind of emotional tug inside: a feeling of pain, anger, or unhappiness.

- Make a note of the feeling next to that name.

- Then write down the reasons you feel that way about those people. Did you never get to tell them how much they hurt you? Did they cause you injury or abuse you in any way, or simply not love you as much as you loved them?

- These notes are important tools for searching your unconscious mind and finding exactly what you've been holding onto emotionally that may be keeping you from giving yourself fully to a new relationship.

Once you've completed this list, review it: Is there any relationship on this list that causes you to have a very strong emotional response? Does thinking about it make you feel extremely angry, hurt, fearful, or out of control? If so, it might be wise to get a professional to help you process these feelings.

If you still have *some* feelings that feel unresolved but not paralyzing, try the exercise below. Even though the person or relationship has no strong control over you, it is still important to get rid of any residue left behind by the relationship. This exercise will help you rid yourself of the remaining negative cobwebs. Read the description and then follow the steps, or have a friend read it to you while you go through the steps. It should take you around fifteen minutes.

YOUR INNER CIRCLE

Close your eyes and imagine a white light of protection surrounding you. Know that nothing bad can enter this white light of protection; you are completely safe.

Now, imagine that you have a guardian angel seated next to you. This guardian can be a real angel, or it can be a beloved family member or mentor—any individual you know who will offer you wisdom, stick up for you, and protect you from harm.

Imagine that there is a campfire right in front of you, burning brightly. It is the campfire of universal truth, goodness, love, healing, and wisdom. When you sit in front of this campfire, you can only speak truth. As you sit on one side of the campfire, imagine that the person with whom you had relationship issues comes to stand on the other side. He is here to listen to you. This will be your chance to say everything you need to say so that you can both heal and move on.

With the white light of protection around you and while you are feeling the presence of your guardian angel with you to help you be strong, tell this person whatever you need to say. You can speak it out loud or simply say it in your mind. Feel free to get emotional during this process: if you're angry, shout out loud: "I am angry!" If you are hurt, cry. If he made you afraid, tell him so. Get everything out of you that you never told him, or you told him and you felt he didn't hear, or you told him and he fought back against. Remember, this is your inner circle, and you must tell him what was really going on with you in the relationship. You may have tried to do this during the relationship. Only this time, your partner simply stands and listens to everything and, perhaps for the first time, really hears you, because you both are within the inner circle of truth: he *has* to hear you. (If he is not listening, imagine your guardian angel walking over and giving him a swift kick, or a pop on the head, to make him listen!) Keep going until you have said absolutely everything you needed to tell this person.

Now, with your guardian angel standing next to your former partner, imagine that it's his turn to tell you what he needs to say—but he can only speak the truth as he saw it. Knowing now how his behavior affected you, he explains why he acted the way he did. If he starts to try to justify or wiggle out of taking responsibility, your guardian angel lays a hand on his shoulder, forcing his to tell the truth. Every word that is said passes through the circle, which means that you hear it from the perspective of eternal wisdom. When we hear others' words in this way, we can see how this person's own hurt, anger, and past issues have created their actions.

Once your former partner is done, it's your chance to respond. Again, say anything and everything you need to in order to feel that this relationship is complete. Give your former partner the chance to do the same, and continue until there is nothing left to say on either side.

Now, ask your guardian angel to say whatever she wishes to add. What wisdom can your angel give to help you heal yourself and move on? Listen to what she has to say very carefully, knowing that she wants only the best for you and is there to protect you and help you heal.

Finally, imagine there is a small, golden box on the ground next to your feet. You pick up the box and open it. This is a special box in which you are to put all your memories and associations from this old relationship. As you hold the box in your hands, imagine that every emotion, every feeling, every memory of this relationship, good and bad, is pouring into the box. Because it's a magic box, it can hold everything no matter how much you put in it. Once you have moved everything into the box, you close the lid, and your guardian angel walks over to you, hand outstretched. You give your angel the box, and she turns and casts it into the fire. As you watch the box blazing in the flames, you feel as if all your feelings and memories are being melted down and refined in the fire of goodness, love, truth, and wisdom. All the bad feelings disappear, leaving only the good memories and the valuable lessons from this relationship. You look across the fire at your former partner and notice how differently you feel about him. If you can, forgive him for the pain he caused you. If you don't want to do that, simply say goodbye, knowing that he taught you valuable lessons that will help you in your new relationship. Watch him turn and walk away from the campfire.

Your guardian angel reaches into the fire and takes out the gold box, which glows with the goodness, love, truth, and wisdom it has absorbed from the campfire. Your angel hands you the box—you're surprised that it is cool to the touch. You open it, and immediately all the goodness, love, truth, and wisdom from the fire, along with all the good memories and valuable lessons from your former relationship, rush into your body. You are filled with the beautiful, loving energy of the campfire.

Your guardian angel smiles at you, knowing that you are healed. You feel ready to move on with your life, ready to share your love, ready to love more fully, wiser and stronger than ever, and knowing that you are always protected by a universe that has your best interests at heart.

Once you have done this process you might want to reinforce your healing with affirmations. It's good to remind ourselves of the universal truth on a regular basis by repeating to ourselves statements like "I am love and protected, and I draw to myself the love that is perfect for me."

Compose a few affirmations for yourself and repeat them when you go to sleep at night and when you get up in the morning. Those moments, when the conscious mind is relaxed, are the best times to program the unconscious mind, which is far more powerful in healing and attracting what we want into our lives.

Your PAST-LIFE *Relationships*

Sometimes our relationship challenges are a result of incidents from lives before this one. My sister Alicia (a therapist, and also a specialist in past-life regression) and I have worked together on many cases in which her clients have brought up issues that originated in earlier incarnations. Such issues can affect our current lives in three different ways.

Past-Life Karma

As I mentioned in the Introduction, we may be dealing with karma we created in past lifetimes. The person that we're drawn to for no particular reason but who turns us down could be the reincarnation of a partner we loved and left in a previous life. Or perhaps we find the perfect person and have a passionate relationship for a few years, only to have that person die or leave or otherwise terminate the relationship. It could be that our karma has been completed, and it's time for this person to move on. In every lifetime we are simultaneously fulfilling our past karma and creating new karma that will affect our next incarnation. Our job is to build up as much good karma as we can by learning, growing, and loving to the best of our ability. However, sometimes atoning for our past karma in this life can create pain and confusion on our part. That's one of the things that past-life regression therapy can help us understand. It can reveal to us what issues we have carried from one life into the next, and assist us in processing those issues as easily and effectively as we can.

Karma and Destiny

The effect that past lives can have is in shaping our destiny. As I said earlier, certain events in our lives are predestined because of our relationships with other souls that last throughout time. We are fated to meet that certain man or woman because he or she is a part of our eternal family, and our destiny is linked to theirs. Renowned psychiatrist and past-life regression expert Brian Weiss wrote an entire book about one such relationship—*Only Love Is Real.* In it, he describes interacting with two separate patients, Elizabeth and Pedro, whom he regressed over many sessions as they relived dozens of past lives. It was only after months of therapy that Dr. Weiss noticed that these two people, who had never met each other in this life, had been lovers in several previous lifetimes. They described the exact same events but from different perspectives, one as the husband who came back to his village to find his family dead and his wife missing, the other as the wife who was captured by a warring tribe and forced to work as a slave for its leader. Was it an accident that these two ended up as Dr. Weiss's patients at the same time? I would argue that they were destined to meet and fall in love, which they did. Their connection over many lifetimes predestined them to come together in this one.

Acknowledging Past-Life Traumas

Our relationships can be shaped by our past lives when we bring to this life the effects of traumas and bad relationships we have experienced in earlier incarnations. Suppose you've always been attracted to people younger than yourself by at least ten years. If someone asks you about it, you say, "I don't know why, but I'm not interested in people my age or older—I just don't trust them." You can't think of any reason in your past that would make you distrust people older than you; it's simply an automatic emotional response.

If you have a past-life regression session, you may discover that in a previous life you were forced to marry someone much older than you, who didn't love you and treated you poorly. You swore that you would never be in that kind of relationship again, but you died before your spouse. In this lifetime you are keeping that promise to yourself. Now, that may be fine—but if traumas or bad relationships from past lives are preventing you from seeking and finding love in this one, it's just as important to heal these past-life issues as it is to heal ones from your present incarnation.

To Summarize

If you believe there may be problems that originate in a past life, I strongly suggest you consult a hypnotherapist or counselor who specializes in these issues. Simply understanding where your challenges come from, whether they are a result of past lives, bad relationships in this life, or problems with your parents or other family members, can help guide you when it comes to your current relationship or the relationship you wish to create.

CHAPTER 6

The Attraction Principles

Once you have gotten whole, clear, and balanced, you're ready to take the necessary steps to start attracting your partner into your life. Before you start your search, however, you need to tap into the power of the universe to support you. You can do this by:

Awakening Your Intuition

Creating a Vision of Your Partner

*Preparing a Space
for Your Partner to Join You*

STEP 1: *Awaken your intuition.*

As I mentioned earlier, intuition is the voice of the divine love of the universe that whispers to us and guides us to make better choices and prevent problems. I believe that intuition can be our most valuable ally in the search for love or to increase the love we already have. But we have to let intuition know that our heart is open for business. In the same way that we can tune in to different channels on the television or radio, we can actively tune our intuition so that it is sensitive to the signals of love that are all around us, allowing us to send and receive those signals to and from potential partners more easily. It's like choosing basic cable or premium channels. We want our converter box to have the highest range of possible vibrations. Intuition can give us information about potential partners that logic and reason cannot, and it can help us become aligned with what the universe has in store for us and show us how we can attract the highest and best into our lives. Intuition can warn us of possible problems in our relationships, too, and help us to see past the surface in our would-be partners to the truth of what lies beneath. It's our own inner GPS when navigating the sometimes complicated map of relationships.

Intuition also can be very helpful when we're getting ourselves ready for a partner. In fact, intuition is often the way we tune in to the blocks and obstacles that have kept us from being happy in our past relationships, and it can help us discover what references may have shaped our present behaviors. Sometimes it's our own intuition; at other times it's the intuition of a family member. Recently I read for a woman whose husband of several years finally confessed that he was gay. As it turned out, her father had picked up on this fact long before but had hesitated to say anything because he knew his daughter wouldn't believe him. In both cases her father was right!

Here are a few quick tips for tuning in to your intuition:

Believe in yourself: You must start by believing that you are intuitive. Everyone has this sixth sense, including you. It's your gut feeling. Once you accept that it exists, you are more likely to see how it plays out in your life. If you don't believe that you have intuition, you're setting up what psychologists call a blind spot. It's like being told to go into the kitchen to find the salt, but because you're so preoccupied, you walk right by the salt shaker several times before you go back to the dining room and say, "I looked—the salt wasn't there." Or, as international motivational speaker and author Dr. Wayne W. Dyer puts it, "you'll see it when you believe it." Believe you have intuition and you'll open yourself to noticing how it is working in your life.

Quiet your mind: Take the time to quiet your mind for a few moments every day. The conscious mind is always busy, always noisy, and it can drown out intuition's more subtle signals. If you quiet your mind, you stand a better chance of noticing what your intuition is telling you. We are constantly bombarded with information and this can seem like a huge challenge, but just "allow" yourself to start with five minutes—even if you have to use an egg timer! After a few days, you will find it easier to take a little more time for silence each day.

Review your past: Look over your past relationships or your life in general and see where you've already been prompted by intuition. Ask yourself whether you followed its guidance or not.

Did a boyfriend or girlfriend cheat on you and you knew about it before they ever said anything? What did you do about it? Did you meet someone and instantly know the person would be a great friend or partner? Did you pursue that relationship as a result? Did you get an intuitive warning that someone would be bad for you but you ignored it and then suffered the consequences? If you look over your life, I'm sure intuition has given you signals that you either paid attention to or didn't. By simply recognizing how your own intuition has tried to help you, you can become more receptive to seeing it working in your life today.

Pay attention to signs: The best way to awaken your intuition is to pay attention to its subtle signals. It can let you know you are ready for a relationship by bringing certain signs into your awareness—a feeling of anticipation, for instance, or a magazine at the doctor's office that falls open to an article on Internet dating. Maybe all of a sudden everywhere you look you see couples holding hands or kissing, or, for no reason, your high school sweetheart (who was your perfect love while you were together) keeps popping into your head, or "your song" keeps playing on the radio. Start looking for and paying attention to the "signs and signals," or coincidences, that are all around you. If you're not quite sure if something is an intuitive sign or just a couple kissing, for instance, ask the universe to make the sign clearer for you. (I usually add, "And if you could make it a pleasant sign, I'd appreciate it!")

When I conduct lectures or have personal consultations about intuition, I always say that intuition will take you places that logic and common sense never can, and that is doubly true when it comes to our relationships. In order to prepare yourself to find and choose a partner and then to create a loving, strong, dynamic relationship together, intuition will help you see beyond the surface to the other person's deepest nature. By making intuitive choices, you can grow closer more rapidly. Take a few moments to recognize your own inner wisdom, to acknowledge it, and to tap into its power. Intuition can be your greatest friend and ally in creating your best relationship.

STEP 2: *Create the vision of the love you want.*

I'm a firm believer in the power of vision. Creating a clear vision of the relationship you want to have does three things:

1. It forces you to be clear about what's important to you in a partner, so that when the person shows up, you can recognize those qualities more easily and get clarity on expectations.

2. It helps you get your priorities straight: you'll know what's essential, what's nice, and what doesn't matter when it comes to your relationship.

3. It's a signal to the universe that you're ready and open for a partner to show up, starting now.

Assuming you've done the inner work we talked about earlier and that you are tuned in to your inner wisdom, you can now ask for what you want clearly. You will now be in alignment with the universe, instead of fighting with it, and with no psychological or emotional obstacles to prevent you from attracting and nurturing a fulfilling relationship.

Creating a clear vision of your future beloved can be an easy and *very* enjoyable process, especially if you allow your intuition and conscious mind to collaborate. While there are many different processes for drawing a clear picture of a romantic partner, here are a few suggestions you may find helpful.

CREATING A VISION

Set aside time to create this vision. It's not something you can throw together, unless you want a thrown-together relationship! Give yourself a couple of hours that you can dedicate to thinking about and envisioning your partner.

Set up an appropriate atmosphere so it will be easy for you to focus on love. Do whatever will put you into an appropriately loving, romantic, and open state of mind and heart. Some people like to light a candle, to sit in a favorite chair, or to go to a favorite spot, like the beach or the woods. Do what makes you feel good.

Bring a journal or notebook that you will dedicate to creating your vision of a partner. I'd suggest selecting one that signifies love to you by its design, color, or composition. On the first page, write your name and then the title of what this journal will describe: "My Perfect Mate," "The One of My Dreams," "My Soul Mate," "My Soul Partner," or whatever means the most to you.

Begin by closing your eyes and saying a prayer or simply expressing your gratitude to the divine for the opportunity to love and be loved. Ask for protection and then request guidance as you create the vision of the relationship that will be perfect for you at this time. Attuning your vision to what the universe wants for you right from the start will help ensure the happiest result.

Now, take a few deep breaths and allow your mind to become quiet. Allow your intuition and your unconscious mind enough space to begin designing your perfect relationship. If you meditate regularly, you might want to meditate for ten minutes or so. If you don't, simply focus on your breathing and let your thoughts come and go as they will.

In this space, with your body and mind centered and calm, ask your inner wisdom, "Who is my perfect partner? What is this person like?" Trust that what comes to you will be the guidance you need. Let thoughts, images, and ideas flow into your conscious awareness, and capture them in your journal. Don't edit— write down anything that comes to mind. It could be that you'll see a clear picture of your perfect partner, or that you'll hear a voice or a name, or that you'll get a sense of what the person's presence will feel like. Whatever it is, note it in your journal. Keep asking "What else?" and writing your impressions until nothing else shows up. When you're done, take a moment and thank your intuition for the information it has provided.

Without reading what you have written, turn to a fresh page in your journal. It's time to involve the other two aspects of your inner wisdom: logic and common sense. Ask your conscious mind to tell you, "What do I want in a partner? What's important for me to have in a relationship?" Write your answers on the new page. Include everything that you might consider when choosing an intimate partner: physical appearance, career, age, character traits, whether he has children (or not), where he lives, what his hobby is, what sports he likes, and so on. Do not edit yourself for any reason. This is not the time to be "politically correct." If hair color or weight or income is important to you, write it down. Once you have your list, look it over and see if there's anything missing—think of it as your ultimate relationship list, and if something's not included, you won't get it in your partner. Keep writing until you can't think of anything else.

Without reading this list, turn to a clean page and ask another, equally important question: "What *don't* I want in a relationship? What are the things that I absolutely will not stand for in someone who is my intimate partner?" Write your answers on the new page. Be brutally honest: it's just as important to be clear about what you *don't* want in a partner as what you do want. Write everything from "must never cheat" to "must not leave clothes on the floor" to "must not have bad teeth" or whatever would drive you crazy. Keep writing until you've put down every possible thing that would make this relationship less than extraordinary.

Now, take a break! Stand up and stretch, get some water, take some deep breaths—do something to change your energy.

Now, read over your lists in order: the intuitive list, what you want in a relationship, and what you don't want. Are you starting to get a clear picture of your future relationship? Imagine how rich your life will be when your beloved shows up!

To make your visioning stronger, I suggest you review your two conscious mind lists (what you want and don't want in your relationship) and prioritize everything you wrote. Write a "1" by the traits or elements that are absolutely essential; a "2" by any trait or element that is important but not essential; and a "3" by anything that would be nice but isn't vital. For instance, if you have children (or want them), you might put a "1" by "must love children" (essential), a "2" by "likes sports" (important but not absolutely essential), and a "3" by "brown hair" (nice, but not vital). On the list of what you don't want, you might put a "1" by "must never be violent toward me or any child" (essential), a "2" by "must not swear" (important but not absolutely essential), and a "3" by "must not watch soccer on TV every weekend" (nice, but not vital). Once you've prioritized your lists, rewrite the list of "1" priorities on new pages in your journal.

Here is the final step, and the most important! Close your eyes and imagine that this perfect partner is coming into your life in the next month. Remember all the intuitive impressions you had of how this person looked, sounded, felt. Imagine how you will feel when this amazing soul looks into your eyes with love. Connect to that vision emotionally, intellectually, physically, and spiritually, and enjoy it. That's the love you desire and deserve, a truly heavenly love that will uplift you both. Remember you are looking for the RIGHT and PERFECT PARTNER—not the same frogs you've been kissing in hopes one will turn into the handsome prince.

With that feeling in your heart, open your eyes. On a fresh page, answer this question: "What kind of person do I need to be in this relationship? What will I give? How will I share myself? What gifts will I bring to my partner?" To attract your best partner, you need to be your best self—open, honest, vulnerable, and strong. You should not try to be anything other than who you truly are. You don't have to be perfect any more than your partner will be perfect—but you can be perfect for each other, in all your beauty and frailty and humanity. Let yourself declare on paper who you want to be for this wonderful partner.

Congratulations! You have created a clear vision for the relationship you desire. I suggest you review this vision at least once a week, right before you go to sleep. You can add to or change it as you wish, but keep it as is for a little while so it can settle into your conscious and unconscious mind.

After you read your vision, close your eyes and put the call out to the universe, letting divine love know you are ready for this person to appear. Be grateful that this person is coming toward you right now. Then go to sleep knowing that, when the time is right, you and your beloved will meet.

By the way, if you are already in a relationship, making these lists can have value for you, too. They will help you become clear about (1) what you love in your partner, (2) anything that drives you crazy that you feel is important to change, and (3) why you want to be in your current relationship. It's always good to reassociate with the person we love. When we take time to remind ourselves of all the reasons we care about them, we can renew our commitment to be our best selves for and with them whenever possible. So start visioning, and enjoy!

STEP 3: *Make space for love in your life.*

Once you've cleared out your mental and emotional closets, gotten in tune with your inner wisdom, and created a clear vision of your partner, it's good to do the same things on the physical plane. This signals to the universe that you are now ready and open for your partner to join you.

You need to actively make space for your relationship. This can mean literally cleaning out closet space so a new love can move in with you; getting your financial and/or career house in order so it will be easier to spend time with your love free of unnecessary worries about money or job; and, often, getting rid of anything that reminds you of past relationships or associations. If you are hanging on to mementos from other loves, how comfortable do you think Mr. or Ms. Right will be coming into your home and seeing your favorite picture of your former spouse over the fireplace or on the bedside table? Even if the objects are not obviously linked to your former relationships, *you* know that they are, and your memories of the old can keep the new from taking hold. So even if that lamp or chair or painting or item of clothing has positive memories for you, put it in storage. Get it out of your living space and let some fresh air in.

You might think of replacing these items with things that signify your readiness for a renewed or new relationship. Basic principles found in disciplines such as feng shui and color therapy, for example, can serve as guides for creating energy that will support great relationships.

- Keep your bedroom for sleeping and . . . you know. No TV, Internet, exercise equipment, or other distractions. And get rid of clutter. Especially under the bed! Do not store any mementos from your past relationships there! Your bedroom should be clean and tidy, ready for that special someone to join you there.

- Make sure there's room in your closets and dressers for your sweetheart's belongings. The bed should be big enough for two and accessible from both sides. (Some feng shui experts advise that if you're currently single and you're used to sleeping in the middle of the bed, start leaving room for a potential partner now by sleeping on one side of the bed.)

- Position the bed so that your feet are either at an angle facing the door or perpendicular to it—do not have the bed in a direct line or opposite the doorway. This helps clear the flow of chi energy and allows free circulation. Make sure your bed is comfortable and inviting.

- The images and items in your bedroom should reflect your openness to a relationship. Pairs of things are great—two lamps, for example—as are artworks that feature loving couples, romantic settings, and so on. Eliminate anything that might remind you of former partners.

- Don't make your bedroom too masculine or feminine. It should be a place where your ideal partner will feel at ease and welcome. Keep colors soft and soothing. If you want to add a little spice, accessorize with a few items that seem sexy to you. Remember, if you're in the mood, your partner is more likely to be in the mood too!

- Get used to retiring at a reasonable hour. Don't stay up working late if you can avoid it. Start preparing for your relationship by spending more time in the bedroom.

- Place the journal in which you described your vision of the perfect partner next to your bed, and read it once a week.

There's an old expression in some personal development circles—"Act as if." It means that if you act as if something has already occurred, you're more likely to be able to create or attract it into your life. There is much being said today about the Law of Attraction, and everything I've mentioned so far is to help bring that "attraction" to fruition. I believe that the effort attracts the results: when we make space in our lives for a relationship, or try to revitalize the relationship we have by paying attention to it and caring for it, and when we prepare ourselves emotionally, psychologically, and physically for greater love, then we are a lot more likely to bring it to ourselves.

If we are in tune with our intuition, we'll recognize it when it shows up and we'll be ready to welcome it! We will be able to expand our lives and embrace and share love with our intimate partner.

CHAPTER 7

Your Action Plan for "Action!"

After we've prepared ourselves to be open to love and be loved, we still have to do the work to find our soul mate. Unfortunately, we can't just put our order in with the universe and expect Mr. or Ms. Right to be delivered to our door! The world today is vast, and we can find our potential partners in many different places: the Internet, dating services, international business contacts, and the ability to travel worldwide make meeting interesting people everywhere we go that much easier. But our ability to connect with so many people also makes finding someone special that much more complicated. Here are some questions that I am sure are rolling around in your head, and some answers. Not to worry, we'll get to the most pressing one—"What do I do next?"— right after the following questions:

- Do you put up a profile on a dating site or go to a singles evening at your local church or other networking opportunities?

- Should you ask your friends to fix you up with possible partners?

- When you do hear about someone interesting, should you call, meet, or email first?

- How long should you be email pen-pals before you speak on the phone or meet in person? Cautionary note: some people like to "hide" so if you want to get the job done, have a real (voice) conversation on the phone sooner than later. It's too easy to pretend you are something you are not when you can manipulate words on a computer screen.

- Should you meet for coffee, dinner, or a movie?

- Who pays?

- Who picks who up, or do you meet there?

- Do you give your date your home address, or do you wait until you make sure the person isn't a nutcase?

- Do you Google your dates? Do you have to do a background check on every potential partner?

Sometimes it's enough to make you long for the days of the 1950s sitcom, when men were men, women were women, the rules were clear, and you had a much smaller dating pool to draw from!

With the new wide-open world of dating, **it's more important than ever that we use our intuition as well as our logic and common sense to help us in the search for possible partners.** When you engage all three of these forces, and you are consciously keeping yourself open to love and to the currents of destiny, you'll be able to make the most of the meeting, greeting, and getting-to-know phase of creating a great relationship.

Getting STARTED *on* *Your Mission*

If you did the exercises from the last chapter, then you have awakened your intuition, created a vision of your relationship, and organized your environment to welcome a new love. Now you're ready to start looking! This can either be a wonderful time or the most painful thing you've ever done, depending on your attitude. If you're smart, you'll look at this period as a time of adventure, research, exploration, and FUN!

To make this process easier and more enjoyable, it's not enough to want a great relationship; you need to prepare yourself by getting whole and healthy. You'll also need an action plan. This starts with internal preparation and then extends to the practical actions you'll need to take to find your ideal partner. There are three steps that will get you ready to enter the great world of dating.

Set a Clear Intention for Your Search

You already have the vision of your ideal partner, which you should continue to review at least once a week. Now start imagining how and when this person will show up in your life. Repeat statements like "I'm ready for my new relationship to appear." (Another suggestion is that you open your bedroom door each morning and yell, "I'm ready!") Be willing to state what you want, when you want it, and how you want it to happen. **Intentions have power,** especially when we set them and then let the universe do its part to make them occur. Remember, you're not in total control of attracting the relationship you want. There are a lot of other factors that come into play, such as cosmic timing. The universe ultimately determines when you will find your ideal partner. The intentions and destiny of your potential partners are similarly out of your hands. **Set your intention, declare it, and then do what comes next without worrying too much about the results.** Try to stay open to enjoying the process. It IS an adventure—perhaps the adventure of your life!

Create a Tool to Help

As part of setting your intention, you may want to create a "wish board" with images and words on it that represent the relationship of your dreams. A wish board is one way to take your vision and put it into words and images, thereby engaging a different part of your brain and creating a concrete vision of your ideal relationship. But one word of caution: I've learned from experience that when it comes to wish boards and the visions, desires, and intentions they illuminate, you must be very careful what you ask for—you just might get it! Be careful, because what you dream may not be what you truly want or need. In addition to giving you an opportunity to illustrate what you truly want, a wish board can help you avoid what you do not actually need. Say you meet someone incredibly wonderful and you put her name and photo on your wish board, but it's not your karma to be with that person. The universe may have someone even better in store for you, or if you had a relationship with this person it would not be healthy. It's your job to evaluate your wish board when it all comes together, and I caution you against including someone's name. This can breed obsession, especially if the person in question is not part of your destiny. The same rule applies for including words like "marriage," "long-term commitment," and other constraints.

For example, for many years I have had a wish board for my own relationships, but I don't put the word "marriage" on it. Instead, I put "loving, warm, healthy relationship" because I'm not interested in any old marriage—I want to make sure that if I get married again it will be a great relationship first and foremost. That's why I tell people to describe the sort of person they believe will be their perfect partner rather than something like, "I want to marry Joe." I tend to write something along the lines of "I wish for the kindest, most loving, and most generous person that the universe wants for me." Instead of asking for a boyfriend or girlfriend, for example, it's better to ask for a kind person who understands reciprocal love—that certain kind of energy that's formed when both partners have the same emotional commitment. What you want is a person you can trust, who will work as part of a team for the well-being of you both. **Be clear on the essential traits you want in a partner, and then let the final product come as a surprise.** Release the wish on your board to God or a higher power and say, "If it's the will of the universe, I will have this kind of relationship or something even better." And always remember the saying, "Man proposes and God disposes."

Unless we seek a past-life regressionist it's difficult to know what our romantic karma is, and whether we are destined to meet the person on our wish board soon—if at all. All we can do is set the intention and then start looking, and have faith that what comes our way will be for our highest good.

I also believe that one of the most important parts of setting our intention is not just adding it to our plan for attracting our partner, but rather using it as a tool for planning how loving we will be to this person.

Remember, the goal of any relationship is for our souls to grow in their ability to love. When we focus on how great it will be to express love and share ourselves with a beloved person, rather than focusing on who this person is and how much we need and want someone in our lives, we are putting out a completely different, positive energy. We become an electromagnetic field of attraction when our energy reads: "I'm ready to give and share love." Who wouldn't find that intention powerfully appealing?

Step Out of Your Comfort Zone

Someone once said that it's unlikely God will have your perfect partner walk up to your front door and ring the doorbell. Usually God seems to prefer that we put in a little effort before She supplies a little help. And often, that effort entails stepping out of our comfort zone and being willing to change our habits and routines. We have to put ourselves out there and do things that perhaps we are not accustomed to doing, like putting a profile on an Internet dating service or asking friends to fix us up with possible partners. After all, when we finally get into a new relationship it's pretty much a given that our comfort zone is going to be stretched massively, so we'd better get used to expanding our options the moment we start looking for a partner!

In order to get out of your comfort zone, you will need to banish any doubt or fear that may have resulted from your efforts. Fears are your worst enemy. They stop you from taking the actions you will need to get yourself into the dating game. Most of us who have experienced our first round of dating, perhaps all the way back in high school, may not have the best memories of the process. It's not easy to put yourself on the line when you ask someone out or accept an invitation. The fear of rejection can stop us in our tracks! It's a circumstance in which we can feel inferior, judged, pressured—all kinds of negative emotions. Is it any wonder that doubt and fear can show up when we decide to start looking for a partner?

BUT these two emotions are not what will attract the healthy, loving person you desire. So if you are getting cold feet, go back and reread Chapter 1 and do the exercises in it to get rid of any old negative associations to love that you still may be harboring. Clear yourself out emotionally, psychologically, and spiritually. You deserve a great partner to love, and who will love you. If you have had trouble attracting partners in the past, remember that was the past—this is a new voyage! You have a beautiful new vessel to sail upon. While it is natural to feel a little fear or a few butterflies (and we'll talk more about that later), push any major doubt and fear aside and know that it's your time. No matter what happens, you are ready to love and be loved.

Put Out the Right Kind of Energy to Attract Your Partner

Remember that last part of your relationship vision exercise from Chapter 6, where you described the kind of person you would need to be in this relationship? That's the kind of person you need to be—long before your partner shows up. **When you walk through life exuding open, honest, happy, excited energy, people are naturally going to be attracted to you both romantically and simply as friends.** You can try this out for yourself. Walk down the street or sit in a restaurant, put a white light of protection around yourself, and then project love to the people nearby. AND DON'T FORGET TO SMILE!!!! Chances are you'll notice a lot of smiles and nods, and perhaps a stranger will come up to you and say, "Excuse me, but don't I know you? You seem so familiar." When we send out the energy of love and openness, we're like a supercolossal magnet drawing like-minded people to us.

Another important component of the right kind of energy to bring to your search is that it signals that you are open and available. This doesn't mean you are making yourself ready to be taken advantage of, but simply that your heart is ready for the universe to bring the best partner to you. You should also remember to eliminate any energy of "needing" a relationship. **You are complete and wonderful just as you are. You deserve the most wonderful partner the universe can provide.** And equally important, you are ready to give and receive love completely, with all your heart, to someone who has your highest good in their heart as you have theirs in yours.

I'm a big believer in continually sending the universe signals that communicate your readiness for a new relationship. I suggest that every day, as you get out of bed, you say to yourself, "Today I may meet my partner!" This statement is a signal to the universe that you are ready and willing for this to occur. Hold that thought throughout the day. Don't obsess about it—after all, you're not the only person involved in making this happen; again, the universe and your potential mate are part of this as well. Simply meditate on the knowledge that you will be ready when the time comes, whether it is in a few minutes, hours, days, or months. **God's time is not our time, but His timing is always perfect.** Trust that as long as you are ready to give and share love, you will find your match. Every day simply brings your lover one day closer to finding you!

Seek and Ye Shall FIND

As I have mentioned, it used to be that the pool of potential partners was much smaller than it is now. We found our lovers in our own communities, through our churches, country clubs, or other social groups, or through friends and family. Today, with the Internet, Skype, webcams, and instantaneous global communication, we can find and maintain love anywhere in the world.

There are limitless possibilities, but they also come with some cautionary tales. I once dated a man who lived over a thousand miles away. I was staying in California, where mutual friends introduced us; he had been visiting from Texas. We spent a lot of time on planes and on the phone, emails, and texting, but in the end it wasn't right for either of us. This can apply to Internet dating. Dating websites can allow you to meet many people, but it can be difficult to correctly read their intentions through the smokescreen of online communication, as I mentioned earlier. When I posted a profile on a dating website, I met some lovely men and went on some great dates, and I would consider my experience very positive. However, as a psychic I can usually sense people's intention when I see their profile or speak to them on the phone, which is a real advantage. While I certainly have made mistakes when it comes to romantic partners, bringing my intuition and psychic abilities to dating has saved me from kissing a lot of frogs, so to speak! And I believe that you, too, can use your intuition when it comes to selecting the people you wish to date.

Cautions aside, I'm a fan of online dating, and dating services, because they open your energy to the possibility of romance. Putting a profile online or signing up for a dating service is a big, bold statement to the universe that you're taking the actions that will help you find your partner right now. It also makes you aware of how many great potential partners are available. It's like being a kid in a candy store: you can browse through people's profiles or watch their videos and see all the different possible matches for the vision you created. You can also assume that the people on the site are actively looking for relationships (unless they're just looking for some fun on the side—again, this is where your intuition can really help you; more on this later).

There's another benefit of online dating and dating services: in order to use them you have to create your own profile. This means that you will need to describe yourself and describe your ideal partner in a very concise way. This forces you to be very clear about what's really important to you in a partner and what you wish to offer a partner in return.

When you choose to contact someone from a dating service or website, what you may be doing is finding a good friend instead of your next partner, and that's fine. Really! I went on a date with a man who I thought would be a great match, but we didn't have enough in common to take the next step into a relationship. The chemistry just wasn't right; however, we talked for hours, and it turns out that he's someone I can see spending time with as a friend. I believe that friendships can enrich our lives as well—and who knows? Your new friend may be the contact that leads you to your perfect partner.

If you decide to use a dating service or an online matchmaking site to look for a partner, I strongly suggest the following:

1. Check out the site or service thoroughly before posting your information or signing any contract.

This is simply good old-fashioned common sense. If the site or service is local, check with your local equivalent of the Better Business Bureau. If the service is online, Google the name of the site and add the word "complaints" to see if there are any negative reviews of it. Also, ask people you know who have used online dating sites or dating services about which ones they have used and what their experiences were like. This is definitely a time to get recommendations and references! Your goal is to find a site or service that you feel will give you the best possible opportunities. A reputable, high-quality site or service usually attracts reputable, high-quality people, just like the ones who will be your potential partners.

However, in making your selection of a dating service or site, make sure to let your intuition have a voice in the selection. Look over the list of possible businesses and see if you are drawn to one provider or another for no particular reason. Look for the little currents of universal energy that are pointing you to a particular service. It could be a face on the web page that makes you stop for a moment, or something in the descriptive copy, or just a feeling you get when you read about the services provided that tells you "This might work." But remember, when it comes to choosing anything, from a dating service to a potential date, use your logic and common sense along with your intuition to help you make your decision. When you combine all three, and you add a little assistance from the universe, you're likely to create good results.

2. Be honest in your profile.

Putting up an airbrushed photo or retouched video may make you look ten years younger or twenty pounds slimmer, but what happens when you meet for your first date and the person sees the real you? In the same way, exaggerating your professional accomplishments or financial success or hiding the fact that you have children will only backfire in the end—unless you want to build a friendship or close relationship on the basis of lies. You don't have to tell your dates every single little flaw—like you enjoy eating crackers in bed or wearing sandals in the middle of winter—but you might as well be honest about the big things if you expect anything lasting to come from this relationship. So make sure you post a recent photo (taken within the last five years), and be accurate about your age, height, weight, occupation, number of children, hobbies, likes and dislikes, and so on.

3. Ask for what you want, and be realistic.

In the same vein, be very clear and specific about the characteristics of the people you wish to date. It's better to ask for what you want and get a smaller number of responses than to write a generic description and then wade through a lot of responses that aren't even close to your desired partner. I suggest you refer to the vision you created in Chapter 6, in particular the traits, characteristics, and features that you consider essential, and use those as the basis of your description. Remember, in looking for a partner, all it takes is one—the right one. In the same way, your potential partner only has one "right one," too—you! Better to ask for what you want and be clear about what you offer; that way you're more likely to find Mr. or Ms. Right instead of Mr. or Ms. "Close-but-no-cigar."

4. Let logic, common sense, and intuition guide your selection of possible dates.

When choosing someone to date or responding to people who ask you out, it's really important to let the three pillars of inner wisdom—logic, common sense, and intuition—advise you. One of the benefits of online dating is that you can learn so much about someone before you ever meet. This allows your logic and common sense to have their say before you get swept up by your emotional or physical response to someone's presence. (That being said, before you meet someone I do suggest that you see a photo or video in order to determine if there is even the remote possibility of chemistry between you. While sexual attraction is not exclusively tied to physical appearance, logic and common sense tell us that physical appearance does play a part in choosing our partners.) I always suggest that you check out possible dates by reading their profiles, watching any videos that they post, and then giving them a call before you meet. Carefully evaluate any responses you get and/or check out any profiles you find interesting before you contact the people behind them.

Pay attention to what people include in their profiles. What do they emphasize? What don't they mention? Do their descriptions of themselves mesh with the important elements of your vision? I'm not saying you should eliminate every person who doesn't match your list perfectly—after all, your list should be guidance for you and the universe. But the perfect person for you could have traits that you hadn't even considered. Just let your logical side and your common sense have their say. For instance, if you have children and the profile indicates someone who doesn't want to date people with kids, common sense says

"Next!" Or if you live in one part of the country and really want to date people close by, logic will tell you to narrow your search geographically. However, logic and common sense should also tell you that if you're so picky that no one passes through your screening process, you'll need to loosen your criteria a little. Mr. or Ms. Right may describe themselves differently than you think they should—give yourself a chance to get to know them regardless.

**The final aspect:
make sure you apply your intuitive sense!**

A good friend of mine signed up for a dating site where you can see who has looked at your profile. One day she had a gut feeling to look at the men who had visited her profile. She noticed one gentleman who looked very nice but hadn't called her. She thought, *What the heck!* and contacted him. It turned out that he had thought she looked far too classy and beautiful to ever want to go out with someone like him, so he hadn't called. They went out, and they continue to date happily to this day. You, too, should let your inner voice have a say in choosing the people you should respond to and date.

When I tried out an Internet dating service, I used my intuition to feel the energy of the people whose profiles I read and who had responded to my profile. I could say, "Yes, no, yes, no, no, maybe." I'd then respond to the yeses, and if a no contacted me, I politely turned him down. But I also used my logic and common sense in choosing the guys I dated. I looked at our common interests, compared their profiles to my own wish board list of important characteristics, and chose men who were in the same geographic area I was. Of course, then I ended up in a long-distance relationship—it just goes to show you that you can plan and choose, but if the universe has other plans, it usually has its way.

One of the best places to let your intuition have its say is during your first phone call with a potential date. (I strongly suggest you talk with someone before meeting—it's yet another means of figuring out if you have any connection without the physical aspect clouding your judgment either way.) Keep the call simple and light. This is not the place to discuss deep issues or reveal your desire to be married within the year. You can tell a lot about someone on the telephone. Check how you respond to this person; do you feel enough interest to arrange a meeting in person? If you do have any questions that weren't covered in the online profile but which are of importance to you, now's the time to ask. For instance, if you would never date anyone who smoked and the profile says nothing either way, you should feel free to ask right up front, "Do you smoke?" Better to eliminate any people whom you would never date with one or two questions than to waste your energy and theirs by going out with them because you didn't ask.

Above all, be open to moving ahead to an actual date unless your logic, common sense, or intuition is giving you a firm "no." Dating allows both people to explore the possibility of a relationship; it's not a confirmation that you've selected the right person from millions of others. I like to apply the fifty-fifty rule when it comes to dating: if I feel more than fifty percent okay about dating this person and he wants to go out with me, then we should set up a date. Even if he's not the person of my dreams, I may make a new friend, or a new business contact, or perhaps find that he knows the person whom I'm destined to fall in love with. Or even if the date just means that I'm putting myself out there, following through with my intention and signaling the universe that I'm ready and open for a relationship, and practicing my flirting and other dating skills, then it will be time well spent.

CHAPTER 8

OMG!
The First Date!

Okay, so you've gone online or to a dating service and found a potentially compatible person. Or you've gotten a call from a friend saying, "I know someone I think you'd really like." Or you've signed up for a singles dance or speed dating or some other event designed to provide an opportunity for singles to meet. Or perhaps you've chatted with someone at church, or at work, or at the gym, or at a concert or other social gathering and you've asked them out or they've asked you out. No matter how it happens, you are now moving from the looking stage to the first date. Now the fun begins—you hope.

Once again, the attitude with which you approach the dating stage in finding a relationship will determine how easy or hard it is for you to connect with a compatible partner.

Dating is a chance for you to try out different people to see if there's a mutual fit. It's a time for exploration, adventure, discovery, and fun. Every date might be the love of your life or an opportunity to learn something important about another human being.

Part of the dating process is discovering what's important to another human being, finding out what her rules are in a relationship and what's important to her, and for her to do the same for you. It's inevitable that you and your date will have differences. **Quite honestly, while your similarities will make you feel close to someone, it's the differences that often make the person interesting.** I always suggest that you approach any date with a sense of curiosity. Think about what you find attractive or intriguing about her. I'm not saying you should look at her through rose-colored glasses and see only what you want to see. It's important to notice any possible areas of irresolvable conflict that will cause you to decide this person is not a good match. But don't let your vision of the "ideal" relationship prevent you from seeing the excellent qualities this person may have. Unless it's clear within the first five minutes that you've made a mistake, give yourself the entire first date at least to learn about her and to let her learn about you.

I mentioned earlier that it's important to be honest when you write a profile or an ad for a dating service. It's just as important to be honest about the things that matter to you on a first date. It's not a time to tell your date your entire life story, but there's no point in lying to him about anything either. If the relationship goes any further, the lies you tell will undoubtedly come back to bite you, and you certainly don't want to start a relationship on the basis of anything other than truth. Better to be honest and have someone tell you "No, thanks" than get into a relationship based on lies. And do try to avoid the "what went wrong with the last relationship" conversation. No need to bring the past into the present. Be here now!

This getting-to-know-you phase is an essential part of any relationship. It's the only way you are going to find a great partner, so you might as well enjoy the process! A date gives you the chance to be yourself and to enjoy finding out about another person. (In my experience, people will usually tell more about themselves on a first date than they will in the three months afterward.) Remember, with a first date, neither of you has much on the line: just an investment of a few hours of your time and perhaps a little money. Make the first date very low-key, either coffee, dessert, or lunch in a public place. That way neither you nor your date will spend a lot, and neither of you has to make elaborate arrangements that could create pressure and make you feel like you have to make this date "work."

Sometimes, however, you may need to go on a date that feels more meaningful. If you're in a long-distance relationship, for example, you may need to travel to go on a date. In that case, you may want to travel to a neutral location away from both of your homes. Or if a friend fixes you up with her brother or sister because you're both in her wedding party, there will be a lot more on the line than just having coffee or going to dinner and a movie because you'll see each other again at the reception. I suggest that in any case you keep your own expectations simple and take the whole thing lightly. If you stay together, any potentially awkward situation will be something for the two of you to laugh about later. If not, you can laugh about it with your friends!

No matter what the circumstances, a first date is an opportunity to see if this is someone you want to get to know better, and vice versa. **If it doesn't click between you and your date, or even if one of you wants to pursue the relationship further and the other doesn't, never consider it a rejection!** You've both simply become clearer about what you want and made yourself ready to move on with that knowledge. Begin the following day by opening the door and yelling "Next!"—knowing that there is another great person just waiting for you.

Remember to engage your inner wisdom (logic, common sense, and intuition) to evaluate your date—and I don't mean do it front of him! Ask your intuition for its input and let it tune in to your companions. Pay attention to the signals that you receive both inside and outside yourself. My friend Bill kept noticing the name Kim on billboards, on store clerk name tags, on streets, on book covers. Then he got a call from his sister saying, "I want you to meet my new co-worker—I think she'll be perfect for you." Guess what the co-worker's name was? Kim and Bill ended up getting married.

On the other hand, imagine that you arrange for your date to come by your house for the first time, and as soon as you open the door, your dog starts barking—and he never barks at people. Maybe your dog senses something that you aren't aware of—yet. Intuition can pick up warning signs that aren't apparent to our logic or common sense and thus can help you avoid painful or dangerous relationships right from the start.

One of the most useful skills you can have when you meet someone is to look beyond the surface and sense the person's energy.

> ### *Here is a simple way to scan someone's energy:*
>
> Put that white light of protection around you; then let your mind go blank and let your energy go out into the world around you, directing it toward your date. It's like extending your nerve endings outside of your body so you can feel the energy of the person you're with. Take note of the first impressions that you receive before your conscious mind can step in.

However, you have to be honest about your first impressions. All too often wishful thinking or sexual attraction can get in the way of our honest, intuitive "hit" about someone. You may not get a lot of intuitive information from your initial scan—after all, every relationship involves getting to know someone in many different ways, and that can take time. But you should be able to get some guidance that can tell you "yes" or "no" or "let's explore this a little more."

You also can set your intention for what you want to sense. Ask your intuition "Is this person's energy positive or negative? Is she honorable? Is her intent pure? Is she honest?" And then read her energy and see what answers you come up with. If you feel unaccountably uncomfortable with this person or you sense a dark energy, dishonesty, or any other kind of warning, be on your guard. If you receive a mild warning from your subconscious when you scan your date's energy, you don't have to walk away at that moment. But be cautious, and ask many more questions before you pursue the relationship further. If you sense danger, however, pull your energy back and feel free to leave. You don't need to have that energy in your life and within your sphere.

Sometimes you're lucky enough to get a clear intuitive signal from the universe about a future partner. When my sister Elaine was newly divorced many years ago, I called her up and said, "I just saw the man you're going to marry. He has dark, curly hair and four kids. You'll meet and marry him in the next six months." Elaine thought I was crazy—she wasn't interested in getting into another relationship, particularly so soon. But shortly after I blurted out my vision, she met David . . . who had dark, curly hair and four sons. They fell in love and were married six months— to the day—afterward! Often people get a "just knowing" feeling when they see someone's photo or skim his bio. I am sure there were times when you were a kid when something went the way you thought it would, and you'd exclaim, "I knew it! I knew it!" That was your intuition, but you probably didn't know it at that time. I'm here to tell you that it's still with you, but probably buried because we're such an "intellectually" oriented society. Those "knowing" feelings are your inner compass.

Once when I was driving to San Diego from Los Angeles (about a two-hour drive) to go to a party at a friend's house, I was stuck in really bad rush-hour traffic. I thought to myself, *Maybe I should just turn around and go home,* but something told me that I had to go to my friend's party. As it turned out, it was at that party that I met a gentleman with whom I had a very intense relationship for about a year.

To determine whether you want your relationship to proceed, I suggest you pay attention to any immediate sense of attraction or "rightness." **There are times when you know right away that**

this is someone with whom you can connect. You may be sexually attracted to him (more on that later), but what is more important is a sense of familiarity, a sense of ease in this person's presence. You may have a feeling that he will be important in your life and, at the same time, a calm knowing that "There's something here to explore." This doesn't necessarily mean that this person is the love of your life. You have free will and ultimately you decide what to do with what your intuition is saying. But it could mean that this is a relationship you should pursue.

Most of the time, a first date is just that—the first meeting. In some cases it will produce fireworks and an instant desire to get to know much more about the person. Or a first date may be just a pleasant time getting to know someone new, ending with a sense that you could enjoy spending more time together. Think of your goal as establishing connection, compatibility, and interest. Even if this person doesn't meet your idea of a perfect partner, if he is interesting enough to want to meet a second time, then that's all that matters. Dates are opportunities to meet great new people. If you want to meet with them again, do so. If not, move on.

CHAPTER 9

Okay, What's Next?

Dating can be an intoxicating time in a relationship. Everyone likes the feeling of pursuing or being pursued, of feeling valued by someone else. Most of us can relish the excitement of a potential new relationship, of the possibility that this is "the one" that we've been looking for.

It's also a time that you can get lost in the intoxication and excitement and forget what you are really looking for: a long-term partner. That's why you need to keep your intuition, logic, and common sense firmly in tune during the first stages of a relationship. If you're interested enough to pursue a second date, now is the time to feel free to check this person out online, on Google or Facebook. Sometimes you can find information that will keep you from going ahead or, alternatively, may confirm that this person could be a wonderful partner.

Intuition can provide guidance, of course, but you have to be careful, because it's easy to confuse intuition with wishful thinking. Say you just got out of a difficult relationship with someone who was very loud and angry. Then you go on a date with a new person who is quiet and unassuming, whose energy is very soothing to your frazzled nerves. Your inner emotional self tells you, "This is exactly what I need!" and because this feeling arises from what feels like your gut instinct, you believe it's meant to be. However, there's a part of you that liked the excitement of the last relationship, and within a few weeks you are bored out of your mind by this quiet, unassuming person. That's just one example of why you must use logic and common sense along with intuition when evaluating potential partners.

If you feel this person is right for you, is there anything else that could be going on? A few questions to ask yourself:

1. Does she remind you of your first girlfriend, the one you never got over, or the parent who never gave you the approval you desired?

2. Are you attracted to this person sexually, to the point where it is clouding your judgment?

3. Is this person available for a relationship—that is, is he currently unmarried or is he already seeing someone seriously?

4. Will it be possible for you both to continue dating with any frequency? Meeting the perfect partner on the last day of your vacation in India when you live in Europe could mean a very protracted and unfulfilling long-distance relationship, which is especially difficult in the beginning stages of creating a bond. That's not to say you shouldn't pursue a relationship if it's not easy to do so, but make sure to consider the input of all three of the pillars of inner wisdom: intuition, logic, and common sense.

The "what next?" phase of a relationship is actually the trickiest, because you and your potential partner have to start navigating a virtual minefield of expectations and rules, as well as the inevitable conflict between fantasy and reality. You will be forced to reconcile your image of your partner with her actual, day-to-day personality, as well as meeting the challenge of incorporating romance into already-crowded lives. I believe the two things that will help you most in this process are your intuition and your willingness to pursue the "getting to know you" process even when it gets rough.

You are moving from your vision of a partner to the reality of Jan, or Mina, or Henry, or Kate. If you are open to it, you will find unexpected gifts in this person, aspects of her life and character that delight you, but you will also find things that do not match your vision and irritate you. The good news is that your potential partner is finding out the same things about you. As you get to know each other, if you continue to call upon your intuition, logic, and common sense, then you'll be doing your part with destiny to move the relationship forward. **Remember, even if this relationship is predestined, there's still free will.** You and your partner have to put in the work to make it work.

WARNING: There is one thing that can get in the way of intuition, logic, and common sense, however, and that's sexual attraction. Chemistry between two people is one of the strongest forces in a relationship. Sexual attraction is not something that we can create by force of will; it's a signal from our bodies that this person is someone with whom we can mate. This signal can appear as soon as you meet someone, or it can develop over time. It can be a signal that you should pursue this particular relationship. It's based on a lot of factors—appearance, masculine and feminine energy, even smell. Old associations can come into play, too—for example, you may be attracted to someone who reminds you of the sexiest kid in high school whom you had a massive crush on.

Your state of mind at any given moment will also have an intense effect on whether you and a partner develop chemistry or not. Have you ever gotten ready for a date, looked in the mirror, and said to yourself, "I look hot!"? Many women I know have certain pieces of clothing that make them feel sexy and attractive, and they make a point of wearing them on dates. This can do a lot toward creating chemistry where otherwise there might have been none. And when you and a date meet and the chemistry starts building, it's great—but it can be powerful enough to blind you to the red flags that logic, common sense, and intuition are waving in your face.

Powerful sexual attraction can really mess you up when it comes to relationships that I'll call "forbidden fruit." These are the kinds of relationships in which you are attracted to partners who are clearly not good for you on some level. This can include people you can't have, who can be more attractive because of their unavailability. Sad to say, we can sometimes be most attracted to dark or trickster energies, so be careful. Remember, Satan was a fallen angel and he certainly has ensnared many a soul over the millennia! Be especially careful if you have had a previous relationship with a dark or trickster energy—this includes situations involving abuse, anger, addiction, manipulation, and so on. Unless you have done the emotional, psychological, and spiritual work to free yourself, you may repeat the pattern again with your next partner. Even a partner who isn't necessarily "bad" could still be bad for you—for instance, in a relationship in which one partner has all the power, or doesn't really care for you, or wants to be in the relationship for a negative reason (security, comfort, someone to boss around, etc).

Do you find that you're attracted only to unavailable partners—those who are married or who live on the other side of the world and with whom you can only have a long-distance relationship? Or perhaps you have fantasized about certain relationships with inappropriate partners, like teachers who fall in love with underage students, or adults who seduce babysitters. When people pursue these relationships and actually get the partner they went after, the result is often a far cry from the fantasy they created in their heads, and they've caused themselves and others enormous harm in the process. Can this be karma from past lives playing itself out? Of course. But I would suggest that in the majority of these circumstances "karma" is mostly an excuse for bad behavior by people who should know better. While everyone can understand the powerful attraction of forbidden fruit, these relationships almost always lead to far more pain than pleasure. If you find yourself drawn to such a relationship, get some help to get over your attraction, because you are undoubtedly setting yourself up for some potentially devastating lessons.

Sometimes the biggest problems emerge when you know the relationship is bad for you, but the sex is good. I think all of us have had the experience of our brains turning off when our bodies turn on. In fact, this is a biological necessity for women—the hormones that rage when we're sexually excited and that allow us to have orgasms also turn off the amygdala, the fear-based response part of our brains. **When you merge with someone sexually, you are taking on his energy and he is taking on yours.** If you are merging with someone whose intent is not good or pure, that can be a big problem, especially for women. In women, having sex activates oxytocin, a hormone that creates feelings of trust and bonding. This is the same hormone that is triggered when a woman has a baby and that builds the connection between mother and child. Therefore, whenever we enter into a sexual relationship, we quickly bond with our partners and trust them. It's a hormonal response that we have no control over, and so it can cause us to bond with partners who we may discover are no good for us.

There's an unwritten rule in modern dating that you should wait until the third date to have sex with a partner. I'm glad that most people don't jump into bed right away, but I think for women it might be smarter to wait even longer before going to bed with a partner. Why? Biologically we are triggered by sex hormones to bond with our partner, and once those bonds are created, they're really hard to break. As soon as women have sex, we feel a connection that may be strictly biological and that may get in the way of our common sense, logic, and intuition. Of course you want to find out if you have chemistry with a potential romantic partner. You want to flirt and feel sexy and be comfortable expressing yourself physically with this person. **But try to keep your brain engaged even when your body is trying its best to take over.** It can feel like you're going against nature to hold back when your hormones are urging you on. But remember that what's more important than sex is to find a partner who is loving and caring, who has your best interests at heart and who will help your soul to grow. Wait on the sex until you are certain about your partner's intent—not just because it's healthier and smarter, but also because you'll have better sex with a partner who is loving and caring.

I feel I would be remiss if I didn't say something about gay relationships, mainly because I still see a lot of pain in people who are gay but unhappy about it. It also causes pain for the people who are in relationships with them—everyone is in denial because everyone is afraid to speak the truth. I saw this pain in the family I mentioned in Chapter 6. This couple was married for years and had two beautiful children. When the children were thirteen and fifteen years old, the husband declared that he was gay. As you can imagine, the wife was shocked—even though her father had intuited her husband's secret—and the couple divorced. In a much sadder case, a young man committed suicide rather than admit that he was gay. He had seemed happy and extremely successful, and he was surrounded by a close-knit circle of friends and family. When his parents came to me for a reading after his death, I picked up on this young man's energy on the other side. "He had a secret," I told them. "I feel confusion about his sexuality—I see him with a woman and then with a man. He felt under pressure to be the perfect man for his family, and he didn't ever want to embarrass his parents. But he was confused and depressed." The young man's suicide devastated his parents, and they also killed themselves. Would these three people still be living if the son had been able to be open about his sexual preference? We'll never know. But I do know that denying your natural sexual attraction almost always creates an enormous amount of pain, confusion, lack of fulfillment, and unnecessary guilt.

I agree with many health professionals who say that we do not choose to be gay or straight, but that we are born with a certain sexual inclination. I also believe that we reincarnate as both men and women in different lifetimes. It's very possible that you might have a soul mate or predestined relationship with someone who has chosen to incarnate as the same sex as you. It's also possible that because you were a man in your last lifetime, you bring that masculine energy into your current life-time as a woman, and your masculine energy still finds women attractive. (Is it really a "gay" relationship when the masculine energy in a woman's body is attracted to the feminine energy in another woman?)

I believe that the key for any successful relationship, gay or straight, is to be honest, first with ourselves, and then with our potential partners, about our sexual orientation. It's far better to find a compatible partner, whatever sex he or she is, than to get into a "correct" relationship that ultimately will be unfulfilling for both partners. If you feel ashamed or guilty about your sexual orientation, please get some counseling to help you understand and accept your nature. You deserve to find a loving partner who will fulfill your needs and desires and for whom you will be the perfect, sexy, wonderful mate—but only if you are willing to accept yourself and be comfortable with the choice of showing people who you really are.

No matter what kind of relationship you are exploring, remember to enjoy the process of dating. This getting-to-know-you-better phase is something you must go through in order to know if this is the partner you want. You'll get to know more and more about him, about his likes and dislikes, what's important to him, and he'll learn the same about you. It's a time when you can feel special, desired, pursued, and you can make your partner feel the same. It's a journey that will tell you whether you two are a good enough fit to pursue a deeper commitment.

CHAPTER 10

Could This Be the One?

Once you and a partner get past the initial few dates and mutually decide that this connection is something worth pursuing, you both begin to move into a dating relationship. This can be an extremely enjoyable time of exploration for you both. Everything is fresh and new, and both of you are on your best behavior. You start experiencing some of those emotions you've read about or you remember from past relationships.

As you spend time with this person, you grow closer. You care about what he says and thinks, and you're thrilled and delighted that he cares about you, too. This is the feeling that everyone wants. It's that time that Byron Katie is talking about, when we fall in love and believe we have found what we've been looking for. **Yet in this phase it's even more important to pay attention to your inner wisdom—your logic, common sense, and intuition—to keep you on the right course and avoid unnecessary pain and heartache—because it's a time when your inner wisdom can stop working.**

Once we fall in love, our ability to think clearly about our partner goes right out the window. The brain center that's involved in critical thinking stops working very well, if at all. We no longer notice a partner's flaws, or if we do, we tell ourselves they don't matter, or, worse, we think *He'll change!* We stop listening to our inner wisdom and hear only the voice of our growing hormonal obsession with the person we are dating.

Over two decades ago there was a memorable commercial on television. It showed a chicken egg, and the voiceover said, "This is your brain." Then disembodied hands cracked the egg into a skillet, and you watched the egg fry as the voiceover said, "This is your brain on drugs." The brain of someone who is falling in love is very similar to the brain of a drug addict. Having sex and spending increased amounts of time together sets off a hormonal storm in both partners that makes you crave each other's company like a drug. In fact, it's been shown that obsession, intoxication, intense hunger and thirst, and romantic love all activate the same areas of the brain. When chemicals like oxytocin, dopamine (which creates euphoria and excitement), estrogen, and testosterone are triggered, you become dependent on your partner to make you feel good: you're like an addict craving the next fix of being close to your partner. You literally can feel withdrawal symptoms if your partner leaves town for even a few days. Often, it's those times of separation when you realize how much you care for—or crave—this person. Your partner's well-being becomes important, perhaps more important than your own.

While this biochemical and sexual bonding is an important part of developing your relationship with a romantic partner, you have to understand the impact of the decision to have sex. Especially for women, if you are uncertain about this person but pressured into sleeping with him or her, the biochemical bonds created by dopamine, estrogen, testosterone, and, most of all, oxytocin—a chemical called the "hormone of love"—can stop you from asking the important questions about the relationship as your body takes over your decision-making. That's why I believe it's better to wait to have sex until you are sure that you are comfortable bonding with your partner.

I know that today there seems to be an unwritten rule among single people that after the third date it's acceptable, and often expected, to have sex. In fact, some people think that sex should be a first step in that it allows you to test-drive the relationship. However, I'm not so sure that's a good rule when it comes to creating lasting relationships.

A friend of mine met someone online and went on two short dates with him (just drinks and lunch—they hadn't spent a whole lot of time getting to know each other yet). On the third date, after dinner, she invited him to her house for coffee. The conversation was still a bit superficial, but, again, they were just getting to know each other. When she walked him to the door, he grabbed her and planted the biggest, soggiest, most unromantic kiss on her mouth. She almost stumbled backward in disbelief! Clearly understanding that she wasn't about to shove her tongue down his throat in return, he angrily said, "I expect sex on a regular basis!" Still stunned, she replied, "Good luck with that. Now get out." She never heard from him again, and she never regretted it. He might have been spectacular in bed, but I doubt it. Making love is not the same as having sex. Obviously he wasn't interested in a relationship...at least not the loving, romantic, and respectful kind.

Once you have sex with someone, it can feel like a magnetic dust has covered you both, pulling you toward each other. Granted, as part of any long-term relationship you will need to explore your mutual sexuality and create a strong attraction and emotional bond. Sex can keep a relationship strong and vital, and it's one of the first places where problems in a relationship can show up. But when you're in the stage of exploring your attraction and connection with a partner, be aware of the power of sex and its ability to turn off your brain completely, deafening you to any guidance you might receive from your subconscious (or your good old-fashioned common sense) about the suitability of this relationship.

Helpful TOOLS for Evaluating Partners

I do a lot of readings for people who want to know if the person they're with is right for them, and many times I can sense if this person is part of their future. A reading with a good psychic or intuitive can alert you to the suitability of the partners that may be coming into your life. There are also other tools you can use to check if potential partners will be good matches for you. Throughout the years I have been fortunate to meet some of the world's most notable experts in astrology and numerology, and I have gotten valuable, accurate advice about the relationships I was in at the time. Tools like astrology and numerology don't necessarily give you specific details like name, address, and phone number, but they can help you see if you will be compatible with a potential partner and help you navigate the more difficult-to-map terrain of your potential mate's intangible qualities.

Once you begin to think that you might want to pursue a serious relationship, I suggest you use these disciplines to check on your partner's compatibility. There are so many intricacies in these practices that when I first started studying them it was like learning a new language—a bit daunting. But as you will see, because practices like numerology and astrology are so detailed and precise, they present an interesting way of discovering the hidden ingredients of your soul and your potential partner's.

Astrology

When I was eighteen years old, I consulted an astrologer who told me that I would be married and divorced when I was young and then married again later in life. At the time I wasn't in a relationship, but by the time I was twenty-one I was married, and then by age twenty-six I was divorced. (I'm still waiting for the second marriage.) Since then I've had other readings with astrologers who have given me insight into how the stars were affecting my life and relationships. Recently I met a remarkable woman who has become a friend—Sandy Anastasi. Sandy has been a professional psychic and astrologer since 1979. She explained how to use astrology to understand and select compatible partners. I asked her to share some basic guidelines that you can use when it comes to evaluating your own partners. (If you want more information, you can check out her website at www.sandyanastasi.com.)

Advice from SANDY ANASTASI:
Using Astrology as a Tool to Help You Find a Good Partner

I believe that astrology is not simply predictive; it is a psychological tool that can help us understand the basics of the human
mind. The moment that each of us is born, the planets are in
very specific positions that tell us a lot about various aspects
of our personalities, character traits, and lessons we will learn
in life. Astrology helps us recognize the differences in the ways
people see and experience the world, based upon the aspects
of their astrological charts. When it comes to romantic relationships, I believe an astrological chart is a better predictor of success than a background check, because an astrological chart
can tell you what kind of person your partner is and whether
you two will be compatible. To use astrology to determine compatibility, you will need to know (at a minimum) your own birth
date (day, month, and year); if possible, the time of your birth;
and the location of your birth. Naturally, you will need to know
the same information for your potential partner.

Most people know that astrology is based on the *zodiac,*
a series of twelve time periods or signs starting in the spring,
beginning and ending around the twenty-second of the month
and lasting approximately thirty days. Most of us also know the
twelve zodiac signs: Aries (March–April), Taurus (April–May),
Gemini (May–June), Cancer (June–July), Leo (July–August),
Virgo (August–September), Libra (September–October), Scorpio
(October–November), Sagittarius (November–December), Capricorn (December–January), Aquarius (January–February), and
Pisces (February–March). Each sign has one of four *elements*
(air, earth, fire, and water) associated with it, each element
representing the quality associated with that particular sign.
Here's a quick guide to the signs associated with different ele-
ments, and a few characteristics of people born under those

signs. You can see that, based on the elements alone, different people perceive the world very differently.

Air: *Gemini, Aquarius, Libra.* These people are intellectual, very social, and communicative.

Earth: *Taurus, Virgo, Capricorn.* These people are grounded, with a strong focus on the material world.

Fire: *Aries, Sagittarius, Leo.* These people are very physical, energetic, and idealistic (sometimes unrealistically so).

Water: *Cancer, Pisces, Scorpio.* These people relate to life through their emotions and have strong intuitive powers.

It's very easy to check basic compatibility simply by knowing your element and the element of your potential partner. For example, if you put air and fire together, air makes fire burn brighter. So there's a natural compatibility between air signs and fire signs. Water and earth together in nature cause plants to grow, so earth signs and water signs are very fertile and creative when they get together. But if you are a fire sign and your partner is water, you will literally feel like you married a "wet blanket." For example, if you're an Aries (fire), you may come up with a wonderful idea only to have your Pisces (water) partner say, "That's great, but how are we going to pay the rent next week?"

A good astrological chart will show you not only whether you're compatible with a partner but also in what areas problems might arise. When it comes to relationships, the four most important things to know for you and your potential partner are (1) your *sun,* which represents who you are, (2) your *moon,* which represents your emotional nature, (3) your *ascendant,* which indicates how you represent yourself, and (4) the *south node* of the moon, which represents any baggage you have brought with you from past lives. The more signs you have in similar or compatible elements, the better your relationship is likely to be. For example, if my sun sign is air (Gemini, Aquarius, and Libra) and your moon, ascendant, or south node is air as well, we'll get along because we will be able to make a connection, one air sign to another. Even if one of these four is in an incompatible sign, the other compatibilities will often make up for it. If you have a moon and south node in fire signs, for instance, and my sun sign is a fire sign but my moon is in an earth sign, we may have some issues come up, but for the most part we'll get along well.

On the other hand, say I'm a double air sign (Gemini sun and Libra moon) and I fall in love with a man who has a Pisces sun (water sign) and Virgo moon (earth sign). Water and earth go well together, so this man would probably get along well with himself. But water and earth have nothing in common with air and air, and so the only way he and I could relate would be through shared ideas (ideas and communication being a strength of air signs). We might be great colleagues at work, even do well working on projects together, but a romantic relationship wouldn't satisfy either of us. When you understand the basics of the four elements and these four aspects of a chart, you can begin to understand a partner's psychological tendencies and how you are compatible or unsuited.

While you can go online and get birth charts done via computer for free, I really recommend going to an astrologer for a personalized reading if you want a detailed, comprehensive compatibility analysis for you and a potential partner. An astrologer will be able to look at your chart and tell you whether you will be a good romantic match with this person. He or she will take the different elements of a chart and combine the information in an intuitive way to help you make sense of this person's tendencies and show you how to create a strong relationship. For instance, I might see that, based on your moon in Gemini and his moon in Virgo, you are going to be driven crazy by the fact that your partner will never, ever clean the bathroom, no matter how much you nag. However, if you have separate bathrooms, you can eliminate this problem and have a great relationship. This is the kind of information you can't find on a computer-generated chart. An astrologer can help a couple know what obstacles to expect and how to deal with them.

In relationships, having a little bit of knowledge about astrology, the four elements, and sun sign compatibility will help you screen potential partners. At a minimum, get your own chart done by an astrologer so you know about the features of your own chart. This will help you find out what you really need in a relationship. Then, if you are interested in someone enough to go out on more than one or two dates with them (and certainly before you enter into a serious relationship), I suggest you get an astrologer to do a chart for your potential partner. It will help you understand this person at a much deeper level, and it can also show you what you can expect from that person, both positive and negative. I believe checking astrological compatibility can eliminate a lot of grief in the initial stages of a relationship and prevent people from making some pretty serious mistakes.

Sandy is a very wise woman who has a deep knowledge of astrology. In the next couple of chapters you'll hear more from her on using astrology to smooth the way if you choose to create a long-term relationship with a partner, and how the movement of the planets throughout your lives can influence the way your relationship grows and changes.

Numerology

I was introduced to numerology by Glynis McCants, who has been a numerologist for more than twenty years, has done over

20,000 readings, and has appeared on dozens of television programs in the United States. Glynis's work proves that the science of numerology can help you find out how compatible you and a potential partner will be in a romantic relationship. Her latest book, called *Love by the Numbers: How to Find Great Love or Reignite the Love You Have Through the Power of Numerology*, is all about this topic. I was very excited that she agreed to share some of her wisdom with you. (You can also contact her at www.numberslady.com.)

Advice from GLYNIS McCANTS:
Using Numerology as a Tool to Help You Find a Good Partner

Numerology is a science based on a system devised over 2,500 years ago by the Greek mathematician Pythagoras, who believed that the vibration of everything in the universe—including human beings—could be expressed through numbers. Numerology states that the numbers that make up our birth date and name are a blueprint that describes important aspects of our personality, character, and life path. Numerology assigns a specific number (from 1 to 9) to every letter of the alphabet, and that's what we use in calculating the numerical value of someone's name. Whenever you calculate numbers in numerology, you add them together until they are reduced to a single digit as a sum. This sum is your life path. For instance, if your birthday is October 3, 1979, you would add 3 (day) + 10 (October) + 1 + 9 + 7 + 9 = 39, then add 3 + 9 = 12, then add 1 + 2 = 3. So in this example, the person born on 10/3/1979 would be a 3 Life Path. Numerology uses your birth month and day (reduced to one digit), your actual day of birth, your full date of birth, and the full name you commonly use to determine the six numbers that provide a blueprint of who you are. Here are the six numbers and what they describe about you. (To find a Pythagorean number chart that will tell you the numerical value of each letter of the alphabet, you can see my books, *Glynis Has Your Number!* and *Love by The Numbers.*)

Life Path: based on your full date of birth, reduced to one digit. Your Life Path is the path that you must follow in order to be happy in this life. It's the most important number in your reading.

Soul Number: the total of the vowels in the name you use, added together and reduced to one digit. The Soul Number represents your inner feelings—what you need to pursue to be fulfilled in your soul.

Personality Number: the total of the consonants in the name you use, added together and then reduced to one digit. This indicates how you present yourself to the outside world.

Power Name Number: the total of your Personality and Soul Number, reduced to one digit. This represents your strength and the focus of who you are.

Birth Day Number: the day you were born. If the day you are born is not one digit, then you must reduce it to one digit. This is how people perceive you.

Attitude Number: the total of the month and day you were born, added together and reduced to one digit. The Attitude Number is what people first register when they meet you.

Each number, from 1 to 9, possesses a unique vibration and energy, and whenever that number occurs in your name or birth date, it indicates specific characteristics that appear in your life. Understanding these differences between numbers can tell you where you may be experiencing inner conflicts or what paths you should pursue to be fulfilled and enjoy your time on earth. Equally important, numerology can tell you how you will relate to others—this is why it can be so valuable in choosing a partner or figuring out how to get along with the one you've got. There are three categories of relationships between numbers.

Natural Match: As it says, these are numbers that have a natural affinity. When two people with naturally matching Life Path numbers meet, for example, there is an automatic connection. According to numerology, there are three sets of Natural Match numbers: 1, 5, and 7 (mind numbers, which are very cerebral); 2, 4, and 8 (numbers that indicate a focus on the business of life); and 3, 6, and 9 (creative).

Compatible: These numbers are like good friends: they describe people who, while not exactly alike, enjoy each other's company. If there are disagreements between these people, they can work them out. Each number has at least two compatible numbers in addition to its natural matches.

Challenge or Toxic: Toxic number combinations represent people who have tremendous difficulty getting along with each other. No matter what one person says, the other will misinterpret it, because they communicate and see things very differently.

Once you've figured out the six numbers of your blueprint (Life Path, Soul, Personality, Power Name, Birth Day, and Attitude), you can compare it to the numbers of a potential partner to see the areas of agreement and areas of concern. (Remember, if your partner is John Doe but he goes by Johnny Doe, use Johnny rather than John to calculate his numbers.) Here are some basic guidelines on what to look for:

The more Natural Match and Compatible numbers you share with a partner, the easier the relationship will be. It's especially good when a couple's Life Path and Attitude numbers are a Natural Match or Compatible. If you have three or more numbers in common, it is considered a soul mate connection. Your relationship will be very deep and you will either love each other madly or come together to learn some very important lessons.

The more Challenge numbers, the more difficult the relationship. If you and your partner have one or two Challenge number combinations, you can agree to disagree. With three Challenge numbers, you're always going to be working on the relationship and it's not going to be easy. If there are four or more Challenge numbers, you're better off walking away, because staying in the relationship is going to be too draining. Your life will be all about the relationship and trying to make it work—and that's not healthy for either partner.

How do people find themselves in relationships where there are so many Challenge numbers? One word: chemistry. When our numbers don't match, often we tend to focus on the physical aspects of attraction. And toxic numbers actually create a lot of sexual heat: you're so different that the relationship is sizzling, almost addictive. If you've ever been talking with someone and you're just not clicking, but all of a sudden you feel their physical energy and you can't keep your hands off them, you've probably been caught up in the attraction of a Challenge number. The problem is that physical attraction can take you only so far. Eventually the lack of communication between people who are toxic to each other will make the relationship difficult, if not impossible. You're better off looking for partners with whom you have fewer Challenge numbers and more Natural Match or Compatible numbers. With them, you're likely to have both communication and chemistry— and the communication will last long after the sizzle of chemistry has become the warm glow of a loving, compatible relationship.

Look to your partner's Challenge numbers for guidance on ways to communicate better in the relationship. Challenge numbers do not mean someone is "bad"; they simply mean that you and your partner are predestined to see things differently. If you use this knowledge to communicate better, even a relationship that might look toxic based on your numbers can be worked out.

Let me give you an example. Say you are currently in a relationship with someone who is a 5 Life Path. A 5 needs freedom and can't stand being controlled. On the other hand, you are a 2 Life Path, which is a Challenge number for a 5. The 2 needs love and wants to be with her partner all the time. (You can see why these two numbers are Challenges.) If you, a 2, want to stay in a relationship with your partner, a 5, you are going to have to be willing to let your partner go and trust that she will come back to you. Your 5 partner also will have to be willing to spend more time with you than she might consider ideal. You both have to adapt to each other's needs. However, numerology can help you see what those needs are and how you can make your relationship healthier and happier.

Numerology can be a wonderful guide to help you choose a partner and create a strong, lasting relationship. It's particularly helpful because it takes the "personal" aspect out of differences. There are no "good" or "bad" numbers, just numbers that are compatible and others that are not. Once you understand where you and a partner will agree and disagree, you can make the choice to work through challenges or to end the relationship and find someone who is more compatible. If you know the name and birth date of a potential partner, numerology will give you a very accurate guide to his psychology, one that can help you both to create a strong, lasting relationship.

Glynis did a reading for me last year, and she predicted with exceptional accuracy the challenges I was having with a current boyfriend. Not too long after Glynis's reading, I left the relationship for exactly the reasons she described. If you want to ensure a compatible, long-lasting, happy relationship, I believe it's important to use tools like astrology and numerology to confirm what your own inner wisdom is saying. When it comes to choosing a partner for a long-term relationship, the more tools the better!

Keep LISTENING to Your Inner Wisdom

Once you decide you have feelings for a partner, it's important to keep listening to the voices of your inner wisdom. It is not easy, because your intellect and emotions may be saying something else, but the universe *will* give you signs that you are on the right track—or let you know if you're on the wrong track and there's a train coming straight at you! The good signs may be that you feel the energy of the person and you can tell that he is a good, honest soul. Or you start to notice coincidences that make you feel that you're with the right person. You're at work and a thought pops into your head—*I wonder what my sweetie is doing*—and the next moment, your phone rings and it's him. Or you surprise your sweetheart by booking a trip to a romantic hotel for a weekend getaway and discover that it's somewhere she has always wanted to go. I believe that the more time you spend with someone, the more you can connect with your intuition, because you and your partner become more relaxed and open in the relationship—as long as you pay attention to the signals you are getting. But if you feel that something's not quite right, even if you can't put your finger on it, keep it filed away for later, and in the meantime, be sure to pay attention if you continue to receive any other signs or feelings of discomfort. We hate when that happens and often make excuses or dismiss our feelings, but it may be the universe whispering to our intuition.

Dream a Little DREAM

Another way intuition speaks to us is through our dreams, which bypass the conscious mind and thus can give us messages we can't hear otherwise. If you dream of a ring, for instance, that could symbolize a long-term commitment, as rings tend to represent weddings in many minds. If you dream that your partner has found someone else, it could be true (and you've picked up on the signals intuitively), or it could mean that there is someone better suited for her or for you. You also should pay attention to other people's dreams about you and your partner. Sometimes because of the fog of romantic love, our intuition can't break through our conscious mind to warn us about a relationship, and so the universe uses another channel to get its message across. A few years ago I dreamed that two of my best friends, who had been in a relationship for twelve years, had split up. The next morning the three of us laughed about it over breakfast. But sure enough, a year later, they separated. My point is that if we can have dreams about other people's relationships, then they could have dreams about our own. So if someone tells you they had a dream about you and your honey, pay close attention. This could be important information that you were not able to see, but the message has been sent.

Occasionally, our departed loved ones will speak to us in our dreams to tell us their opinion of our current relationship. Maybe right before you go to sleep, you think, *I wonder what Grandmother would think about Joe?* Later, you dream about your grandmother, who mentions that she likes your new boyfriend.

Keep a pen and paper on a bedside table so you can capture any impressions from your dreams, especially dreams that feel psychic. Psychic dreams are often particularly vivid, and the best time to capture your impressions is just after you wake up.

However, although we may be able to record the contents of our dreams on paper, interpretation is often more difficult. A sign you receive in a dream may be a signal from the universe that this is the right relationship for right now, but it may not be a sign that it will last forever. Or perhaps the universe knows that this is a great relationship, but psychologically it's the wrong time—maybe your partner is just getting over a bad breakup. It is important to contrast positive signs with reality, which requires combining intuition with common sense.

Wishful THINKING

Also, remember that wishful thinking can block the honest signals of our intuition or cause us to interpret them in the wrong way. In my last relationship, I kept getting signs that I interpreted as signals from the universe that I was supposed to be with this man. Once, when my boyfriend and I were in my apartment together, I was singing, "Goodnight, My Someone." Something told me to turn on the radio. Five songs later, the station played the same song I had been singing! I thought, *I guess I'm in the right movie!* However, my desire for lasting love was influencing my interpretation of this sign from the universe. It wasn't that this was a relationship that would last; instead, it turned out to be a karmic relationship that I had to go through in order to learn some important lessons.

Wishful thinking can also cause us to believe the exact opposite of what the universe is really trying to tell us. When I was in college I dated a guy seriously for a year. Then we broke up. I didn't see him for six months, but he was still all I could think about. Then one day I had a feeling that I would see him that day. I took a shortcut that ran behind a local bowling alley, and there, driving toward me, was my ex-boyfriend! He jumped out of his car and waved to me to stop. He told me he loved me and missed me and that we needed to work things out. I'll admit I'm a romantic, so I guessed that this was fate: we were meant to be together. He wooed me nonstop. Eight months later we were married—and five years later, we were divorced!

Looking back, I believe that our meeting didn't mean that we were destined to marry. It was simply my psychic ability combined with my desire to see him that caused me to drive down that particular road. Even if we were destined to meet that day, our relationship wasn't written in the stars. It was always up to me to choose what I would do after that meeting.

Not everything is predestined, and all of us have free will and choice, especially when it comes to relationships. We have to do our best to notice the signs we are given and then interpret them correctly.

"Houston, We Have a PROBLEM*"*

Intuition can be especially valuable when it warns us of things that can cause us pain or are dangerous. A few years ago my friend Celia went through a pretty bad breakup with a man who had pursued her persistently. She cut off all communication with him and asked him not to contact her again. This gentleman lived in another state, so she thought she wouldn't have to worry about seeing him. However, one morning when she was getting ready to leave town for a weekend trip with friends, she got an intuitive "hit" while she was in the shower: *That guy is in the hotel down the hill from me!* Dripping wet, she called the hotel and confirmed his registration. Then she left town with her friends. When she got home on Sunday, she found half a dozen messages from this ex-boyfriend asking where she was and if he could see her. Her intuition had saved her from a potentially difficult situation.

As your relationship develops, keep checking in with your inner wisdom. If something continues to bother you, follow up on your feelings. More important, if you ever experience a fear that can't be explained by logic or common sense, something that seems to come from deep within, put a white light of protection around yourself—imagine that you are a lightbulb shining at full power—and ask your intuition to tell you what's going on. You could be getting a warning about possible danger.

The most important thing to remember is that *you must be willing to walk away if the relationship becomes unhealthy.* This can be difficult when you've spent time with a partner, bonded with her emotionally and sexually, introduced her to your family and friends, and incorporated her into your life. However, for your physical, emotional, psychological, and spiritual health, it might be necessary to leave. Condoning bad behavior or allowing your boundaries to be crossed won't make you happier or your partner a better person. All it will do is set you both up for a very unhappy time. I'm usually an eternal optimist in most of my relationships; I tend to work on myself to fix things that cause me problems. In the past I've stayed in relationships because I had the illusion and the Pollyanna attitude that I could help the other person. I've also spent way too long watching a partner "try" to change, only to have him fall back into his old ways. Don't let yourself be fooled by someone who is charming and persuasive and knows you well enough to push all the right buttons to keep you. If you can logically see that this person isn't healthy or isn't really a good match for you, be willing to walk away immediately.

Sometimes we can get sucked in by the romance of being pursued. A psychologist once told me that many people go back to or stay in unhealthy relationships because their partners pursue them so strongly; these people have a need to feel needed. The attention is flattering, almost addictive, and it sucks them back even though they know the relationship is bad for them. It's important to look past the pleasurable feeling of being desired and pursued to the actual experiences in the relationship that are unacceptable. You, or a good friend, should do a reality check on the relationship to figure out whether it is good or bad, and if it's bad, you need to have the strength to leave.

The point of dating people is to discover who they really are and to see if you are a good match. In some cases, you will find out that you don't share enough to make your connection into a long-term relationship. Be honest enough to break things off. It may hurt. You may go through withdrawal. You may be lonely and berate yourself for screwing up again. But truthfully, you simply found out that this person wasn't a good long-term fit. When you leave a relationship that isn't working out, you allow yourself and your would-be partner the freedom to find the person who is right for each of you.

On the other hand, you may find yourself being left instead of leaving. This is usually harder, as you may still have feelings for your former partner. Do yourself a favor and just let this person go. Don't keep chasing him, or you might end up like the women in *He's Just Not That Into You*, fruitlessly obsessing over partners who have long since moved on. Let go and don't judge yourself. You didn't "fail" in the relationship—you just weren't a match.

The most important question to ask is always, "What did I learn?" Every relationship that comes into our lives does so because there is some lesson we need to be taught, and especially when the lesson is painful, we want to learn it once and once only! Learn your lesson, mourn the loss if you must, then go back to your vision and revise it based on what you have learned. Then, when Mr. or Ms. Right does show up, you'll be ready.

CHAPTER 11

The Relationship Evaluation Quiz

Remember that in addition to intuition, you can use logic and common sense to help you assess your relationship at every stage.

Here are a few (but maybe tough) questions to help you evaluate and assess the quality of your developing relationship. You should take this quiz periodically and see how the results match up.

1. **How does this relationship make you feel?** Do you feel happy? Do you feel more like yourself? Is this someone who inspires feelings of both love and friendship in you?

2. **What's your energy like around this person?** Do you feel light and bright? Has your world expanded because you are with her?

3. **Are you great together?** Do you feel like you are better together than you ever were when you were apart? Does being together bring out the best in you both?

4. **Do you feel that you can be completely honest with your partner,** even if you have something difficult or unpleasant to express?

5. **Do you feel you are stretching and growing in good ways?** Are you both more loving because of your time together? More caring? More open? Wiser? Happier?

6. **Does this person love you the way you are?** You should feel that you can be yourself completely, not who he thinks you should be.

7. **Are you comfortable physically with each other?** If you're having sex, is it satisfying to you both? Are you enjoying exploring your sexuality as a couple?

8. **How is your partner fitting in with your family and friends?** Are you happy with your partner's family and friends as well?

9. **Are you a good match?** Do you feel that you complement each other in outlook, taste, energy?

10. **Will this relationship make both of you happy in the short term and long term?** Can you foresee a positive future with this person?

Conversely, here are some questions that will help you determine whether this relationship is *not* the one of your dreams.

1. **Do you feel less like yourself around this person?** My friend Maggie was in a relationship in which, as her friends told her, the man she was seeing dimmed her light because he was so needy. Feeling that you are less than your best is a big red flag.

2. **Do you feel drained energetically when you're with this person?** You may have attracted what my colleague Judith Orloff calls an "emotional vampire"—someone who sucks the energy out of you and gives almost nothing in return. Or you may have fallen for a narcissist who cares only for herself. Often these people are extremely magnetic and attractive, but they're just not capable of real intimacy. If your partner makes you feel drained rather than energized, he is not for you.

3. **Do you believe you have to change in order to be "good enough" for this person?** We all may need to alter certain things to make room for a new partner, but you should never feel you have to change in order to be "good enough."

4. **Do you feel that you have to walk on eggshells?** You shouldn't feel that you have to be supercareful of a partner's feelings, either because he'll become angry or hurt or because he'll abandon you. If your partner is noncommunicative or if you have to struggle in order to have a serious discussion, you're always going to have to work too hard to stay connected.

5. **Do you ever have the sense that you're being manipulated?** If you feel that you're being manipulated, especially for your partner's selfish reasons, don't walk—run! He may be in the relationship only for what he can get from you, not because he wants to give.

Part of the process of creating a relationship is "living and forgiving": being together, learning about your partner, discovering each other's good points and imperfections, being flexible, and forgiving what's minor while holding the line on what's truly important. However, true love can't be blind—in fact, it needs to see very clearly in order to decide what's important and maintain that standard.

Setting boundaries and knowing your bottom line are absolutely essential in creating a healthy relationship. You need to know what you will not tolerate in a partner and make that clear to her. You also must make it clear what the consequences will be if she violates an important rule, like sleeping with someone else—and then keep your word and leave the relationship if she does. In the same way, however, you need to recognize similar boundaries and bottom lines for your own behavior. In a relationship, turnabout is always fair play. You should never expect a partner to follow your rules if you aren't following them yourself. Indeed, if you find yourself breaking your own rules, it's a clear sign that you are not with the right partner.

CHAPTER 12

Act Naturally and You Can Be Committed

If you're attracted to someone and that person is attracted to you, that's great! Now is the time to enjoy the process of finding out more about each other. Think of it as an adventure! You will both unveil your likes and dislikes, your common interests, your values, your differences. All these discoveries will add spice to your relationship.

As you spend time together, you'll either become closer or grow further apart, and your attraction for each other will increase or decrease. Don't try to force growth by being overeager, and likewise, don't be standoffish to keep your partner intrigued. Let the energy develop between you in its own time and its own way. Try not to play mind games—with yourself OR with your potential partner. Remember that all the traps set by your past relationships need to be far behind you, especially the traps you set for yourself!

Be aware that you and your partner may feel different levels of closeness at different stages in the relationship. You may be ready to see each other every night of the week while your partner feels that's too much too fast. Or your partner is already picking out the china pattern and you're still deciding if you want to invite him to spend the night at your place!

The expression "timing is everything" really applies at this point, and a mismatch of timing and expectations is one of the main reasons that relationships falter, especially in the beginning. Always remember that your partner needs to process this new relationship in his own time and own way, just as you need to. Give him his own space and don't be afraid to ask the same for yourself. Above all, be cautious of any expectation of a long-term commitment, in your conscious or unconscious mind—this can definitely put a strain on the natural unfolding of a relationship.

Enjoy this getting-to-know-you phase for what it is, and trust that time and your partner will show you whether this relationship is for the short or long term. If you have begun thinking of your partner as your boyfriend or girlfriend or significant other or some other term that indicates you've moved beyond seeing each other casually, eventually one or both of you will start to wonder whether you should make a long-term commitment: move in together, get married, or formalize your civil union. This step will either evolve naturally, with both of you coming to the realization together, or one partner will suggest some action. I believe the timing of this decision is very important, because it's all too easy to rush in and make something permanent that in reality could use more time to develop. When we are in the throes of the high provided by the combination of dopamine, estrogen, testosterone, and oxytocin, we'll pretty much do anything to keep experiencing that high, including making long-term commitments to partners who ultimately are not right for us.

Are You COMMITTED?

There comes a point at which the drug high of attraction wears off, and in its place we develop a new, more sustainable chemical balance. We produce less dopamine, which creates excitement and the sensation of a drug high. I mentioned earlier that when we have sex we produce oxytocin, the chemical that produces feelings of bonding and closeness. Now is the time when you want to pay attention to that feeling—not after the first sexual encounter! Couples no longer need to spend every moment in each other's company, but instead have forged emotional bonds due to shared experience and caring. This stage of a relationship is designed to be sustainable over the long term, allowing partners to maintain a comfortable emotional relationship. This enables them to welcome others—that is, children—into the family.

To reach this stage of emotional comfort with a partner takes time. The best relationships are those in which a long friendship has followed the initial period of attraction—a period of time that allows you to truly get to know each other before committing to anything permanent.

Most therapists are of the opinion that it takes an average of three years for partners to really get to know each other in order to create a lasting relationship. It gives them the opportunity to observe each other and participate in a variety of activities or crises.

It's a temptation to believe that "omnia vincit amor," or "love conquers all"—a phrase from Virgil's Tenth Eclogue—suggesting that if you love each other enough, it doesn't matter how long you've known each other. But taking time to really get to know a partner, "warts and all," is time well spent. You can't truly know someone unless you've seen that person in many different circumstances—the normal and abnormal, the highs and lows of life. It's always better to wait a little longer and be absolutely sure than to rush into a long-term commitment and then later end the relationship with a painful breakup. If it's meant to last, it will—and you both will be stronger for it.

Waiting also gives you both an opportunity to get used to being a couple. Every relationship is a new entity, something different from the two people who compose it. "Chris and Dan" are different from Chris the doctor and Dan the professor. As a couple, people will relate to you differently. You will enjoy life differently and experience it in different ways. You will find different challenges together than you would have if you were single. And with each new challenge, you'll see a different side of your partner than you did before.

Only after you have spent time together and have seen your partner's best—and worst—aspects will you know each other fully. And the more time you spend with your beloved, the more opportunities you'll have to watch your partner change and evolve as you change and evolve. Give yourselves the luxury of a grace period in your relationship: a time to explore things together before you take the next step into a more permanent commitment.

This grace period also gives you a chance to figure out the areas in your relationship where you'll both have to change in order to make it work in the long term. Look carefully at what you need to do, what you need to let go of, and what will make you and your partner happy. Don't change your core values or your goals—if something is truly important to you, you have a responsibility to express your needs and desires and, likewise, to allow your partner the freedom to do the same.

Through an open dialogue you can work out issues to your mutual satisfaction as you learn the skill of compromise.

CHAPTER 13

What If We "Have Some Issues"?

It's inevitable that "stuff" will come up between any two people. The ways in which you both deal with these issues will tell you a lot about the staying power of your partnership. Becoming aware of how a partner copes with stress and confrontation can actually draw you closer. When you become accustomed to dealing with issues together, you'll no longer feel that you have to be on your best behavior all the time; you can let your loved one see you as you are, even in challenging times.

There are five primary categories of "stuff" that can arise in the dating phase of a relationship and that must be handled prior to any long-term commitment.

CATEGORY ONE:
Baggage from Past or Present Relationships

Most people bring some sort of baggage with them: some have carry-ons and some have steamer trunks. You or your new love could come from a family with a history of alcoholism or genetic propensities to certain diseases. Perhaps there are past financial issues that may affect the new relationship, or there may be a child or an elderly parent with behavioral, physical, or psychological difficulties that you or your partner must cope with. In today's world, where divorce is common, you may very well be dating someone who has children (or you have children yourself), and they come with visitation rights, ex-spouses, and a variety of child-rearing issues. No one enters a new relationship completely baggage-free.

Sometimes baggage will doom even the most promising relationship. A man came to see me for a reading because he was afraid his fiancée was cheating on him. His first wife had left him for another man and, since that time, he suspected every woman he was with of cheating. Until he got rid of that emotional baggage, I told him, it would be next to impossible for him to have a healthy relationship. Another couple explained that, although they are deeply in love, both of them have had such bad relationships in the past that they're terrified of making any kind of commitment.

It's up to you and your partner to (1) be honest with each other early in the relationship about any past baggage that may affect you both, and (2) decide how you will deal with that baggage. In the case of the people I just described, I suggested that they get couples counseling. If you are dealing with any kind of baggage, seeing a therapist or counselor together and separately may very well help you dump some of the weight of your negative associations and allow you to commit fully to creating a healthy relationship.

In some cases you just need to be willing to take on each other's baggage. My nephew, Lenny, married a lovely woman whose daughter is severely autistic, and watching how wonderful he is with his stepdaughter, Jocelyn, is a real inspiration. He knew going into the relationship that he was taking on a lifetime responsibility in Jocelyn, and he was happy to do so. Today his family life is full and fulfilling for everyone: Lenny, his two sons from a previous marriage, his wife Robin, Jocelyn, and her two sisters. Sometimes you will learn the value of a potential partner by the person's ability to work through the unavoidable difficult issues in a relationship. No matter what, it's important to acknowledge each other's baggage and, if you want to continue the relationship, figure out early on how to deal with it.

CATEGORY TWO:
Relationships with Friends and Family

Many people feel a need to consult with their loved ones before making a commitment to a partner. They check with parents or other significant family members. If they have children, they consult their kids. Remember that just as you are taking time to develop your relationship with a partner, your friends and family may need time as well. Listen to their concerns, if any, and pay attention to any intuitive response you may have to their feelings. Sometimes friends and family will see things in our relationships that we can't, especially when we are in the throes of our sexual, hormonal urges. This is normal. We want to see the best in the situation—hence the saying "Love is blind." Listen to what they have to say. You don't have to act on it, but pay attention.

My friends will usually tell me exactly what they think of my boyfriends, and I rely on their outside eyes to see what I can't. If what your friends and family are saying is true, your intuition will often back them up. But if their concerns seem minor or may be a reflexive suspicion (which may mean that your friends and family just need more time to get to know your loved one), do your best to allay their fears and keep listening to your own inner wisdom.

You'll encounter one particularly sensitive issue when you meet your partner's children, if he has any, or when you introduce him to yours. How you treat the kids is often one of the most important tests of a relationship. I've found it's best to ask your partner what the best approach will be with his children. If you're making the introduction, share some hints for getting along with your kids. Of course, no matter how much you and your partner agree about this all-important aspect of the relationship, the kids have a lot of input too! Especially when children are young, they can see a new person in their parent's life as a threat. They're also usually very aware that if Mom or Dad has a new romance, the kids are going to have less of the parent's attention. Just as you have to allow your partner time when it comes to growing closer in a relationship, it's important to give your children the same courtesy. Some kids will take to a new person quickly, while others will need a lot more time and reassurance. Just remember, your partner is a package deal, as are you—and your children, families, and friends are all part of the package. You simply need to be willing to work on creating a relationship that will be the best for you, and then do your best to include families as well.

CATEGORY THREE:
Long–Distance Relationships

Nowadays, particularly with the advent of easy long-distance communication via the Internet, it's very common to fall in love with someone who lives in another town, city, state, country, or time zone. Long-distance relationships can be very romantic, filled with longing, intense desire, countless phone calls, explosively sexy trysts, and sweet-yet-painful goodbyes. The problem with these relationships is threefold:

First, when you're separated by space and time, it's all too easy to fall in love with a figment of your imagination rather than a real person. Instead of living with your lover, you're both living in a fantasy world. When your beloved is on the other side of the country, you remember only what you love about him and forget anything that drives you crazy. That's the nature of infatuation, but it has nothing to do with real love or real life.

Second, the problem with long-distance relationships is that you may think you have known this person long enough and well enough to know who she is, but in fact you may have spent only a very short amount of time together—it just seems longer because it's been spread out. In the two years you've been seeing this wonderful person, you actually may have been together for a total of eight weeks: three passionate weeklong vacations, ten weekend trysts, and two weeks' worth of family holidays. That's not a lot of time to get to know a possible long-term partner.

Third, the challenge is that neither of you has had to incorporate this relationship into your everyday life. You and your lover have completely separate lives. You have no idea how he will handle having to clean the kitchen to your standards, or whether she'll respect your financial priorities. You've never had to work out all the little, important aspects of an everyday relationship—aspects that you are going to have to deal with if you want the relationship to go any further.

The bottom line is that long-distance relationships are closer to fantasy than reality. If you're going to pursue a romance with a partner who lives far away, eventually someone's going to have to move so that you can get to know each other in the real world.

CATEGORY FOUR: *Romance versus Reality*

Maybe you've been flattered and entranced by the delicious feeling of being pursued by a lover who will do anything to make you his. But once you're caught, your lover no longer has to pursue you—on both sides, the thrill of the chase is gone, and romance starts to give way to reality. You may start noticing that your beloved is not exactly the ideal of your dreams, and the course of the relationship isn't following the idealized path you created in your head. Instead of delightful weekend getaways and clandestine lunchtime trysts, you're figuring out what to do with your lover's kids over the weekend and trying to schedule dinner together in between business trips and long days at the office. You've morphed from a lover into a boyfriend or girl-friend—you're more of a sure thing now, but you may feel a loss of excitement and variety.

We all get caught up in romance—the songs and presents and special pleasures that are part of the sweetness of a new relationship—and it's wonderful to be desired and to desire. But when we're emotionally involved, we can be charmed into seeing what we want to see rather than what is. That's why moving from an unrealistic romantic "high" to reality is often the best thing that can happen when it comes to evaluating your partner as a potential lifetime companion. While you can keep the romantic fires burning in a long-term relationship (as we'll discuss in the next chapter), you'd better take the time to discover whether you can live with his socks on the floor or her habit of grinding her teeth, or the fact that you like football and your partner prefers Mozart. When it comes to figuring this out, earlier is better than later. You need to see the red flags before you make the commitment, so it will be a wise decision that you will not regret. You must learn to love not the romantic ideal you've created, but the flesh-and-blood person you have attracted, and your potential partner must do the same.

CATEGORY FIVE: *Fear of Change*

I think most of us would love it if we could incorporate a partner into our lives and never have to make any kind of adjustment— but as we all know, that's the biggest fantasy of all. Relationships bring change: that's part of their purpose in our growth and development here on earth. To be in a relationship, we must let go of certain aspects of our lives. We can no longer be completely independent. We will have to consult someone else's needs and desires when we make many decisions. You may want to take a trip to Spain in the summer, but your honey is going to have the kids the entire month of August and they always go camping in Germany every year. Or your partner would prefer to stay in most evenings, but your job requires you to entertain clients at business dinners three nights a week. Sometimes the little things can be the hardest to change. Your mom always cooked with wine and your sweetie is a teetotaler. You've always slept on the left side of the bed but so has he, so someone's going to have to change sides.

Any of these changes, whether they are small or large, can provoke all kinds of emotions in both parties, including the fear of losing yourself in the relationship. You have to look carefully at what choices you'll have to make and decide when you should compromise and when you should ask your partner to change. It's better to set your pattern of discussion, compromise, and clarity early, because your ability to know when to bend and when to stand firm is an essential element of a healthy long-term relationship.

Whenever issues come up, remember that as long as you and your partner both love and trust each other and you approach your relationship with the commitment to work things out, you can overcome most obstacles. If both of you are sincere and have the right intentions and put your relationship first, and if your inner wisdom is continuing to tell you that this is the right person right now, then be willing to do the work to keep the relationship healthy and strong. If you do, both of you are likely to keep loving and growing, and that's what relationships are all about.

CHAPTER 14

Wait! Before You Commit, Ask Your Intuition!

Committing to a partner is a big step, so consulting your intuition beforehand is a wise decision. In previous books I described a specific form of "intuitive asking" that works well when it comes to questions like "Should I commit to this relationship?" or "Should I marry my partner?" Let me give you a short version here for you to use as part of the process of making a commitment to a partner.

Intuitive Asking

STEP 1: Create a clear, specific question.

Ask "Should I marry X?" or "Should X and I move in together?" Don't ask something fluffy and unclear like "Should X and I take our relationship to the next stage?" The more specific your question, the clearer the answer and the easier it will be to understand.

STEP 2: Clear your mind, focus on the present, and get ready to listen.

Find a peaceful, quiet environment free from interruptions or distractions. Have paper and a pen ready to capture any messages you may receive. Sit down, get comfortable, and close your eyes. Visualize a white light around yourself and say a prayer of protection. Take a few deep breaths, and then bring your focus completely to the present moment.

STEP 3: Put all emotional involvement aside and ask your question.

Desires and wishes can block intuition, so ask your question without emotional attachment to a specific reply. It can help to put your question in the third person: If your name is Mary and you're dating Thom, you'd say, "Should Mary move in with Thom?" Ask once, and then wait for an answer to come to you.

STEP 4: Pay attention to what you're getting.

Take note of the first thought, image, sound, feeling, or impression that surfaces in your mind. Don't edit or try to interpret—it may take a day or so for what you've received to make sense. Sometimes your answer will be a clear "Yes" or "No." It also could be a positive or negative feeling, or a symbol, or a noise or vision. It's also possible that you may not get an answer right away. Often our intuition has to sneak past the conscious mind to communicate with us, so your answer may come in a dream or when you're not focusing on your relationship. Maybe you aren't supposed to know the answer right now. If that's the case, then thank your intuition, and keep asking it periodically for signs. Remember, however, that you must be prepared for an honest answer that may not be in accord with your wishes and desires. When you ask the universe a question, you'd better be ready for the truth.

Asking Permission from Departed LOVED *Ones*

If people have lost a previous love to the other side, it is often difficult for them to accept a new relationship in their lives. They may feel that they are "cheating" on their departed loved one. Client after client will ask, "Does my first husband know about my new boyfriend?" "Do my parents like my spouse?" "Does my wife on the other side approve of the way my second wife is raising her children?" I think the real intent of their questions is not to seek approval, but to be reassured that their loved ones on the other side are still with them and still care about the people here on earth.

A couple of years ago a friend of mine requested a reading for her dear friend, Marje. Marje's husband had died several years earlier and she had recently found a wonderful new man, Michel, but she wondered what her first husband might feel about the new relationship. Her first husband quickly came through to reassure her. I told Marje: "His name is Jacques, correct? He says you still talk to him. He misses you and he will always love you. But he's happy about your relationship with Michel. In fact, he's telling me he knew Michel in other lifetimes and has a karmic debt to him. It's almost as if he is giving you to Michel. And he's happy that you're so loved, both here and on the other side." I find that our loved ones in heaven want us to find love again when they are gone.

One of the more poignant readings I did was for Miranda, a young girl from The Netherlands, who had fallen in love with Louis, a handsome American, when she was living in New York. After she had returned to Europe for a short while, intending to go back to New York, she got a message that Louis had been shot to death at a nightclub. She came to me for a reading because she kept dreaming that her boyfriend was very upset and she was afraid he was angry at her.

I reassured her: "Absolutely not. Louis says that he's upset because it was a stupid way to die. He asked you to marry him, right?" Miranda nodded. "He meant it—he's showing me a heart and pointing to the necklace you're wearing and saying, 'That heart is from me.' He gave you the greatest gift of all: to prove to you that you could love someone and he could love you back. Now that you know how to love, he wants you to take all the love you had with him and share it with somebody else. He says that your heart is big enough both for him and for a wonderful new man who's going to come into your life." This reading gave

Miranda a great deal of healing, and I have no doubt that she will be a beautiful partner for a very lucky man.

Our departed loved ones will often give us signs that they are with us as we pursue relationships. Maybe you're driving, thinking of your dad and hoping that he would like your new partner, and one of your dad's favorite songs comes on the radio. Or your first wife always loved bluebirds, and when you start dating your current girlfriend you notice bluebirds outside her apartment all the time.

Remember, however, that we keep our personalities when we pass over, so you need to take that into account when it comes to your departed loved ones. If your wife or husband was jealous in life, they may not be eager to see you with someone new. If your father, mother, friend, or sibling was controlling and manipulative, their advice from the other side may be designed to continue to control and manipulate you now. Whenever you ask for anyone's opinion, always consider the source and check the answer against your own inner wisdom. It could be that your karmic lesson is to stand up for yourself, to finally step out of this person's shadow and do what's right for you. Check what you receive from your subconscious against your inner knowing, as well as your logic and common sense, and then proceed with faith that you are doing the best you can.

CHAPTER 15

The Dos and Don'ts of a Long-Term Relationship

Making a long-term commitment should be a significant decision, one that involves intuition, but also your logic and common sense. We talked about creating a bottom line and boundaries for your relationships. When it comes to long-term commitment, your standards are even more important, because they will be the standards you and your partner will live by for a long time, perhaps for the rest of your lives.

Here are some key dos and don'ts for creating a fulfilling long-term relationship. I've learned these from my own relationships as well as by observing inspiring partnerships in my family, friends, and clients. The following are the qualities you should look for:

The DOS

Trust: Trust between partners is the most important quality in any relationship. Trust and love go hand in hand. Trust needs to be earned throughout your courtship. Once you've lost trust in a partner, it's very difficult to gain it again. If you trust that your partner's intent is pure and you believe that she has your best interests at heart as you have hers, then you can enter fully into the relationship.

Respect: This also must be earned. You must respect your partner and his commitment to your relationship. When you disagree, you must communicate based on the belief that you intend to create the best outcome for you both. Respect is vital when it comes to your differences. You must respect your partner's right to his own views, interests, and goals, and he must respect yours. Sometimes you must agree to disagree. You both must also have self-respect, the kind that will not allow your partner to put you down or hurt you intentionally, and won't let you get away with doing the same to him.

Truth: Truth is the foundation of any successful relationship. You and your partner must feel open to be completely honest and frank with each other. You need to be willing to look at your potential partner (and yourself) with honesty, to see both good qualities and weaknesses, and to love both. At the same time, you must tell the truth about issues in your relationship that are creating distance between you and your loved one, even if they are painful. Be honest and get things out into the open.

Responsibility: When you make a commitment to a partner, you are declaring that you are responsible to her and she is responsible to you. This is a promise to care for each other and to care for the relationship. You will be together in both good times and bad, and you're committing to supporting her growth as she supports yours.

Friendship: It is vital to have a partner whom you both love *and* like. You should be good companions, enjoying each other's company and sharing common interests, core values, and philosophies of life. Certainly the differences between you and your partner add spice to the relationship, but common ground makes things easy and fun. All the qualities you value in a friend—loyalty, good company, concern for each other—you also should value in your partner.

Giving and receiving: When a man who had been married for fifty-four years was asked about his secret for a great relationship, he said, "Give sixty percent and expect forty percent." In truth, any time you start measuring who's giving more than the other, you're in trouble. Love is giving and receiving: giving with an open heart and receiving in the same way. If you're giving much more than you are receiving, you need to find a better balance, but in general when both partners commit to giving to and receiving from each other, the result will be a rich and loving relationship.

Kindness: This is not only an underrated virtue, but also an essential part of any enduring relationship. Be kind to your partner and treat him the way you would like to be treated. (Or better yet, find out how he would like to be treated and do that.) Legendary psychic Edgar Cayce described another way to be kind: Minimize each other's faults and magnify each other's virtues, not just with outsiders but with each other. Look for reasons to love your partner, and see his small faults through the eyes of kindness.

Acceptance: When my sister Alicia asked our mother what her secret to life was, Mom said just one word: "Accept." In relationships, as in the Reinhold Niebuhr prayer, you need to learn acceptance of the things you cannot change, courage to change the things you can, and wisdom to know the difference. By "acceptance" I don't mean accepting bad conduct or lying or cheating or anything else that would harm you. Learn to choose your battles wisely, and follow the advice in the title of Richard Carlson's book, *Don't Sweat the Small Stuff*. And don't think you can cause your partner to change. Spiritual teacher Don Miguel Ruiz says that trying to change a partner is like trying to turn a dog into a cat. The only person you can change is yourself. You must love your partner exactly as she is in this moment. Accept her idiosyncrasies and peculiarities for what they are: part of what makes this person uniquely lovable.

Humor: Humor is a healing force; being able to look at your relationship and ask, "What's funny about this?" has gotten many a couple through some very rough patches. Approaching a serious commitment with a light heart can provide balance and joy to both people, making for a lot of fun through the years.

If those traits are the dos for a great relationship, there are also some very serious don'ts. If you encounter any of these things in your relationship, they should warn you away from seeing your partner romantically, much less making a commitment to the relationship.

Major DON'TS

Abuse: Accept no forms of abuse: verbal, physical, emotional, or otherwise. Some people who are charming at first can be hiding the capacity to abuse. And, unfortunately, any kind of abusive behavior rarely gets better over time and usually gets worse as the abuser gets more comfortable in the relationship. If you see anything in your partner that even hints at abuse, leave.

Lies: If you were to ask people to name the one thing that would cause them to break off any relationship, the top of the list would be lying or deliberate deception of any kind. I'm not talking about a social white lie, but when your partner conceals important aspects of his life or personality, it means trouble. Someone who lies easily is not going to be honest in his relationships, and you will never truly be able to trust him.

Giving too much or receiving too little: In a relationship sometimes you will be giving eighty percent and your partner will give twenty, and other times the balance will shift the other way. But if you feel that you are always giving without any kind of reciprocation, move on. Healthy love enjoys giving and receiving. In the same way, if your partner isn't responsible for her part of the relationship, or she feels she needs to take on all the responsibility and thus control you, you're never going to have any kind of equal partnership. This doesn't mean that each of you has to do the dishes or make the same amount of money or divide the chores down the middle. But it does mean that neither of you should feel that you are being taken advantage of.

Selfishness and/or narcissism: I have said for years that selfishness is the kiss of death in a relationship. Each of us needs to have our needs met: that's not being selfish—that's just healthy self-love and self-respect. But when your partner always puts his needs before yours, if he doesn't take your needs or opinions into account, and if he assumes you will cater to him because his requirements are more important than yours, that's not the kind of partner you deserve.

⁓⁓⁓⁓⁓⁓⁓⁓

Once you have set your boundaries and found a partner who has the qualities of trust, responsibility, friendship, truth, respect, kindness, acceptance, giving and receiving, and humor, you are ready to choose this person as your partner for life. And then, if you're lucky, your intuition chimes in and gives you the universe's blessing. It's the moment when you "just know" this is the person you want to be with forever.

Often this moment will have little drama or excitement. It's just an inner certainty that tells you that you have found your partner. You feel you can be yourself completely with this person. The exception is that you will want to be your best. In your relationship, it will be a challenge to continue to be true to yourself and your goals, as it will be for your partner. However, you know that life means change, and you're happy to do what will make your relationship stronger, because you know your partner is doing the same for you. **Ultimately, you must remember that any long-term commitment is a leap of faith in which you declare to the universe that you wish to journey with this partner and grow together in love.** When you choose to walk beside a lover, to be there through good times and bad, to give the best of who you are and to ask the same from your partner, and to love each other even when you're not at your best, you're creating the kind of relationship that can last beyond this lifetime and be a model of love for the angels.

CHAPTER 16

Let's Stay Together: What Does It Take?

Once you take the big plunge, whether it's putting on the wedding ring or moving in together, the relationship is going to change, as will both of you—hopefully for the better!

Now for the tricky part: we've established that problems arise when reality messes up your fantasies. The challenge is to get past the myths of relationships, just like the myths surrounding the concept of soul mates. If you've come this far and your relationship is strong, you will be able to overcome these myths, and you will be able to create a lasting and loving partnership.

Dispelling THE MYTHS

MYTH 1: The purpose of a long-term relationship is simply to love and be loved.

The purpose of a relationship is to *learn and grow* in our ability to give and share love. Growing should be one of your primary goals as partners. There are always new levels of love, caring, passion, empathy, and connection that you and your partner can create. Growing together should be equal to love in your list of relationship priorities. You've probably heard this statement from friends, or maybe you've said it yourself: "We've grown apart." That's not growing. That is more like suffering.

MYTH 2: Your partner should be everything to you.

No one should have to bear the responsibility for being another person's "everything." If I hear someone say that, it makes me wonder how healthy this person is emotionally. It sets up a harmful dependence and creates neediness on one side and resentment on the other. A saying in ancient Chinese culture describes being in a relationship as holding a dove in cupped hands. If you hold on too tightly, you will kill the dove and lose the thing you wanted most. Hold your partner and your relationships tenderly, but with room for both to breathe and grow.

MYTH 3: Relationships should be fifty-fifty.

No relationship is exactly fifty-fifty all the time. There will be situations when you will put in more time and effort than your partner; at other times it will be your partner's turn. Sometimes you're the rock and the stability in the relationship, and at other times you're the one who needs support. This is natural and normal and actually helps you both create a sustainable partnership. More importantly, as I have mentioned, if you are measuring how much each of you is putting in at any given moment, the relationship is in trouble. Keeping score is a game people play because they are insecure. The implied question is, "Do I love you more than you love me?" If you feel you've been giving a lot more than your partner has, you need to do something to address the imbalance. Often your partner has no idea that you feel this way. At the time she may simply need to put a lot of time and energy toward something other than the relationship you share. That doesn't make it right, but it does make it understandable—and negotiable. Communicate!

The only "percentage" that really matters is the part of the relationship that you're responsible for: you. You can't be responsible for your partner's thoughts or emotions. You can't control what your partner says or feels or does. You need to give him the respect and space to take care of his part of the relationship as you do yours. Don't measure how much you are giving versus what your partner is giving. Simply give from a place of self-love and self-respect. When you do so, you won't be allowing your partner to take advantage of you, nor will you feel a need to measure how much or how often you give and receive.

MYTH 4: You know your partner very well; in fact, she's kind of predictable.

Even if you and a partner are together twenty-four hours a day, no one can ever truly, completely know a partner. That's part of the beauty, mystery, and challenge of a relationship. Do you truly know what your partner feels or what makes her feel loved? Are you sure about her likes and dislikes? I read a story about a woman who made oatmeal every morning because she thought that's what her husband liked for breakfast. One day she looked in the cupboard and discovered she was out of oatmeal. Very apologetically, she made her husband fried eggs. "I know you'd prefer oatmeal," she said. "On the contrary," her husband replied. "I hate oatmeal—the only reason I ate it was because you made it for me!"

We want to do things for our partners that make them feel loved, but we often make assumptions about what they want and about whether we've succeeded or not. And then we assume that our partners will continue to feel the same way forever.

Human beings are creatures of change and variety. Yes, we are "creatures of habit" as well, but not everything falls into that category. If you ever assume that you know what your partner wants, you stop being present and aware of what is actually going on. The only assumption you should ever make is that relationships are always changing and unpredictable. Think oatmeal.

MYTH 5: Your partner knows that you love her.

It's very easy to take long-term partners for granted. We stop saying "I love you" because we assume they already know it. We don't make little romantic gestures anymore. Our relationship is now about stability and commitment—the fire of love has become a warm glow. While there's nothing wrong with that, if you stop feeding the fire, eventually it's going to go out! You have to stoke the relationship with attention, caring, selflessness, fun, surprise, and let your partner know how you feel about her every day.

Many people seem to believe that commitment makes it okay for love to be implied rather than stated or affirmed by our actions. Relationships become stronger only if we make the time to express our love to our partners: by word and deed, physically, emotionally, and psychologically. If we're really smart, we'll figure out exactly what makes our partners feel totally loved and surprise them with it as often as we can. Expressing your love is always a nice surprise!

MYTH 6: You should love your partner no matter what.

Until we meet in heaven, we live in an imperfect world with imperfect people who are sometimes not good for us. There's nothing wrong with setting boundaries and having standards. You should expect your sweetie to respect you and not be hurtful or deliberately cruel, deceitful, or overly needy. Love your partner, yes, but love yourself as well, and love him enough to expect him to treat you with the love and respect you deserve.

MYTH 7: If things get rough, it's best to cut your losses and leave.

It used to be that people who married took their vows very seriously, not just because they were vows but also because divorce was socially and financially painful. Unfortunately, today it seems very easy to say "I'm out of here!" at the first sign of trouble rather than devote the time (and sometimes hard effort) to address the problems. Many people think that the grass is greener on the other side of the fence—until they jump the fence and discover there's just as much crab grass with their new partner.

A committed relationship should mean a serious commitment that we do our best to keep. All relationships require work and often sacrifice. There will be times when we will have to put our own personal needs and preferences behind the requirements of the relationship. We must be willing to make someone else's needs as important as our own. When pain and problems arise, we have to deal with them instead of running away. Of course, there are circumstances when it is appropriate to leave a relationship, and only you and your partner can determine if you have reached that point

Relationships are like birth: messy, painful, a lot of work, but hopefully the result makes everything worthwhile. What if in the middle of giving birth, your mom had said, "This isn't worth it—I'm out of here!" As silly as that sounds, I sometimes think we do exactly that with our relationships. We've got to care enough to hang in there, do our best to work things out, deal with challenges, grow and learn and love, and believe that it all will be worthwhile.

TUNING IN TO *Your Partner*

One of the benefits of a long-term relationship is the way we can become attuned to our partner intuitively. This experience is the result of a high level of intimacy of mind, body, soul, and spirit. It is the ability to tune in moment by moment to someone's feelings and needs, almost before that person knows them. Your sweetie walks through the door and instantly you can read his energy and know if he's had a good day or if something's wrong. Our intuition will often signal problems through the body—we'll feel agitated, upset, or just slightly "off." In many circumstances, intuition is doing us a big favor by bringing up something that's weighing on our partner. Maybe there's an issue at work that your significant other doesn't want to burden you with, but you can *feel* his energy change; you can sense his discomfort.

Intuition can often warn us even before something becomes a real problem, allowing us to deal with it quickly and easily. Sometimes all it takes is a compassionate partner sitting down and saying, "Look, I know something's bothering you; please tell me about it—I want to help." When you offer your support in this way, you are giving your partner permission to share what's going on, and you are letting him know you are there for him emotionally. Certainly there will be times when your partner may be in denial or become defensive and insecure when you ask what's bothering him, especially if he feels he should be strong enough to deal with the problem alone. Men tend to have a much more difficult time experiencing their emotions than women—let alone talking about them. However, when we ignore important issues, that uncomfortable feeling from our intuition won't go away. At such times, intuition can be a relationship-saving skill, because it reminds us to deal with an unstated issue, perhaps before it becomes a much bigger problem.

In long-term relationships, it becomes easy not to bother listening to our intuition. Sometimes you come home and all you want to do is have dinner and go to sleep. Even if you sense something going on with your partner, you might just be too exhausted to address it. But that touch of intuition is like the first leak in the roof—if you don't do something immediately, you could be in for a big flood.

We receive intuitive warnings for a reason, and we ignore them at our peril. Don't discount your feelings or compromise your own inner truth to avoid rocking the boat. Intuition can bring up the small problems early so you can handle them. If you wait too long to deal with lingering issues, they can overwhelm even the strongest relationship.

Communication on OTHER Levels

Intuition is one way to tune in to a partner, but the best way to keep the relationship strong is through direct communication. Communication must start from a mutual desire to connect rather than separate. Even the small, seemingly unimportant kinds of communication—questions about your partner's day, stories about yours, a discussion about something you saw or read, a question about what you should fix for dinner—create a web of caring and love that will strengthen your relationship. When we stop communicating, our relationships weaken. Stop for long enough, and it's hard to get that loving feeling back again. That's why I said earlier that we must tell our partners we love them on a regular basis, no matter how long we have been together.

One of the advantages of a long-term relationship is that you develop a common language. After a while you start to know your partner's thought patterns as well as your own. If you're smart, you'll adjust your communication so that your partner can hear what you have to say easily, without becoming defensive. Let's face it—if you go to another country you can't expect people to understand what you are saying if you are speaking a different language. It's important to establish a means of communication.

A friend of mine tends to be cautious and likes to think things through before she says yes or no. Her partner, on the other hand, likes to be more spontaneous and go with the flow. When they first got together, there was a lot of stress in the relationship until they figured out that their styles of communication were different. Now, whenever my friend's partner proposes a plan, he'll say, "I'd love to go to the seashore this weekend. Think about it and let's talk later." If he had said, "Hey, let's go to the shore! I'll start packing!" she probably would have responded in a defensive way, but he has learned to give her the "space" she needs to consider a proposed plan, thus preventing an argument and additional stress.

What are your patterns? What are your partner's? Do you know what he needs in terms of communication? Does he expect you to share everything with him, or would he consider that overcommunicating? What are his rules for disagreements?

Some partners come from families where "spirited" discussions (i.e., arguments) were the norm. Family members said what they needed to say—at the top of their voice, if necessary—cleared the air, and everyone was happy. In other families only "reasoned" discussions were permitted: they talked things out quietly and logically and reached a civilized conclusion. Now, imagine you come from one kind of family and your partner comes from the other. Can you see why it would be important to set some communication ground rules?

And remember that we don't just communicate with words. The tone we use, as well as our body language, can send a clearer message than what comes out of our mouths. Think of the last time you were angry with your partner, and you said something like, "I'll see you later" or "Can you pick up the dry cleaning?" Was your tone of voice different than it would have been if you were feeling loving? Maybe as you left that day you closed the door a little more vehemently than usual—don't think your partner didn't notice—maybe not consciously, but subconsciously. Words are very important, but the other ways in which we communicate often tell the real story of what's going on inside.

Good communication must include being honest enough to ask for what you want. Your needs are as important as anyone else's. You must be willing to get rid of any hidden agendas, be honest with yourself about what you want, and then be brave enough to share those desires with your partner. Some people find this process very difficult. They're afraid that placing demands on a partner (or even making requests) will drive him away. But if your relationship is that fragile, it isn't going to stand the test of time anyway. Your needs have to matter as much as your partner's, and you both must feel free to ask for what you want. But you both also have to feel free to say no to your partner's request. No one likes to be told no, but not granting a request should never be seen as a threat to the relationship. In fact, a dishonest "yes" can stress a relationship far more than an honest "no." Your relationship should be strong enough for you to hear an honest "no" from a partner and feel no loss of love. This is easier when the "no" is delivered with kindness—for example, "Honey, I'm so glad you asked me to go with you on your bowling night, but I'd rather stay in."

Truthful communication will draw you closer. Telling the truth to yourself about your emotions, needs, desires, and problems is the basis for telling the truth to your partner, which gives him the space to tell the truth to himself and to you. Truth becomes magic when it is delivered in an atmosphere of trust. When communication is based on truth, trust, and kindness, you have created a foundation for a legendary relationship that will stand the test of time.

HANDLING *Misunderstandings*

Most of our problems start with either misunderstandings or mis-communications. You say, "I'll see you later," and your partner hears, "I'll be home at six." Then, when you show up at seven, she's furious and you can't figure out why. How many times have you taken something your partner said the wrong way and been upset or offended as a result? It's all too easy to misinterpret what other people mean. Most of the time our intent is not to hurt or upset our partners; in fact, it's often the opposite. But all it takes is the wrong word, or a sharp tone of voice, or even the fact that we're feeling sensitive at the moment, and what was a casual remark or joke can start an argument.

Have you ever been so irritated at life in general that your sweetie says, "Have a good day, dear," and it annoys you? And it's worse if you're already upset about something. Say your partner was in a meeting that ran long, so he was thirty minutes late to dinner last night. Today he says, "Don't forget to pick up the dry cleaning," and you turn on him and snarl, "Look, *I'm* not the one who's unreliable! I said I'd pick up the cleaning, I'll pick up the cleaning!" as you storm out the door. Do you think your partner's intent was to anger you, either by being late for dinner or by reminding you about the dry cleaning? No. But you turned those two things into a major issue. Maybe you were really upset at your partner, but weren't brave enough to tell the truth.

Miscommunications often take the form of indirect comments, offhand remarks, implied requests, and other *I don't want to say anything obvious but I want you to know I'm upset* kinds of stuff. Many people blow up over the little things rather than bring up the big issues, but if those issues aren't addressed, partners are going to keep blowing up unnecessarily and over the wrong things, confusing each other and putting stress on the relation-ship. **It's the things that are left unsaid and unrecognized that can cause the most pain.** Better just to be honest and bring the issues out into the open.

Our work is to *know ourselves* to the best of our ability and be as clear as possible in our communication. Being dishonest or keeping secrets from a partner will always create separation. Even if a partner doesn't know you are lying or keeping a secret, she will feel it on some level, simply because you are not being open with her. Don't keep secrets in your relationship—it's just not worth it. Nor is it worthwhile to hide your feelings or to be dishonest. Respect your partner by being honest with her, and allow her to be honest in return.

> Know yourself.
>
> Be yourself.
>
> Tell the truth.

There is a saying that there are three sides to every story: yours, mine, and the truth. Unfortunately, when we only see our side, it's far too easy to miss the truth completely. We will never see eye to eye with a partner on everything, but how we disagree often makes all the difference. We must respect a partner's right to have his own opinion, and we must never intentionally hurt a partner when we disagree. Unfortunately, as many people have noticed, the greatest irony is this: the people we hurt the most are often the people we love the most. When we let someone into our heart, we also open ourselves up to hurting them, or being hurt by them, whether intentionally or—hopefully—unintentionally.

In relationships, sometimes people feel they don't have to censor their feelings: they can be cruel or mean or angry as long as they are being honest. Personally I think that's a crock and an excuse for lazy communication. Is it important to be honest? Of course. No relationship should be built on lies, and it's better to be honest about the things that bother us than to let them fester. However, there's being honest, and then there's being cruel. Intent does matter, especially in intimate relationships. You can be honest *and* loving, honest *and* compassionate. Treat others in the way you wish to be treated, and bring up difficult subjects with as much understanding and compassion as you can. Here are three things to think about when you communicate:

Is it true?

Is it kind?

Is it necessary?

My sister Alicia describes one way to communicate that combines honesty with compassion and love: always start with an "I" message. Instead of saying, "You were late again—how could you do that to me?" you say, "I feel stressed and upset when you are late for dinner and don't call." An "I" statement becomes an expression of what's going on inside your heart instead of an accusation that makes your partner defensive and angry. Once you've communicated your feelings, give your partner a chance to respond, and listen to the answer. It's just as important for your partner to feel heard as it is for you to express what you're feeling. Once your partner has responded, you can follow up with a request: "In the future please let me know you are going to be late, so I won't worry. And if it gets too late I may start without you." This request includes (1) what you will do, and (2) what you expect of your partner.

Above all, give your partner the benefit of the doubt. Even the most loving expression can be taken the wrong way. Don Miguel Ruiz advises that if you find yourself in the midst of the consequences of miscommunication, ask yourself, "Am I communicating out of love or fear?" Love communicates directly, honestly, and compassionately. Fear is indirect, dishonest, and worried about losing the relationship. **Decide to communicate from love, give your sweetie the benefit of the doubt whenever possible, and you'll find that you'll be able to clear up many miscommunications or avoid them altogether.**

Relationships THROUGH *the Years*

Everything in nature occurs in cycles, and it should be no surprise that the same is true with our relationships. Sometimes you feel as if you and your partner are completely simpatico. And at other times you wonder, "Who is this person and why did I ever think I loved him?"

You may have heard of the "seven-year itch," the point after seven years together at which some people believe that a couple is most likely to break apart. It's not unusual for our biochemical attraction to diminish as time passes by. For whatever reason, in every relationship there will be highs and lows, smooth and rough patches, and how you get through them—or don't— will test you both. I think that, unfortunately, far too many couples give up too quickly and break up over what is often a transitory problem. With the many distractions that are available (dating sites and social networks), there is an illusion of easy "availability" and escape. Sometimes people will want to quit on a relationship and think *Okay, that's it: I need to find someone else to be in love with* when they should be focusing on the positive reasons they got involved with their partner in the first place. However, it's a natural phenomenon for us to drift apart and then come back together—each of us has our own life-cycles that can distract us or pull our attention in different directions.

If you're working overtime at the office or if you have to travel away from home for a few months, it's normal to lose some feelings of closeness with a partner. And when children arrive, it's normal for the child to become a primary focus, often to the detriment of the parents' relationship—it's tough to be starry-eyed while taking out the garbage or changing a diaper. It can be hard when you're in the throes of a major rough spot to believe that this, too, shall pass—but sometimes that's the best thing you can think. **The key is to recognize that such cycles are part of life.** A rough spot shouldn't provoke a temporary separation, and the lowering of the fire of love is not a reason for breaking off a strong relationship.

Relationships change as partners grow and evolve, and it's very easy to get caught up in the drama. Always remember that what seems horrible today may resolve itself next week, or next month, or even in the next moment. Winter is followed by spring. Cycles take us back to where we started. Many people who are in love reach plateaus, but by working on the relationship they often find that they fall deeper in love through the years.

My parents were like that: after forty-six years together they loved each other completely. If you're willing to keep doing the work and love your partner through the tough times, then you will find your love continually reawakening and renewing itself, just as tulips bloom each year after being buried in the snow.

So how do you keep your connection with a partner healthy and vital through the years? Here are some tips gleaned from talking with therapists like Alicia, from observing great long-term relationships, and from my own experience.

• Give each other at least four hugs a day. Physical closeness activates oxytocin, the bonding chemical. Making time for at least four hugs every day will create healthy levels of connection between you and your partner. Plus, it feels good!

• Anger and resentment between partners are wasted emotions, and if you hold onto them, they can be toxic to your relationship. Recognize the issue that is bothering you, express it, forgive your partner, forgive yourself, and move on.

• Overlook each other's imperfections. Recognize that you are both okay just as you are. Be willing to agree to disagree. Appreciate each other's differences as well as your similarities.

• Work on yourself—it's the most important thing you can do to keep your relationship healthy. A partner will see you as you see yourself, so do what you need to do to have a good self-image.

• Work on things together. When you and your partner share goals and face challenges as a team, it can make your relationship even stronger.

• Look at your partner through the eyes of first love. Remember why you fell in love and tell him so. Express your love often. Praise him and offer positive reinforcement and encouragement frequently.

- You should do your best to discover your partner's "love language" (as author Gary Chapman calls it) and use it to make her feel special. One of the most important things you can learn about your partner is what makes her feel completely loved. Some people need to hear it, and others want to see a loving expression in your eyes. Others only feel love when they're touched. Still others need loving gestures, or gifts, or some kind of special treatment. You can do all of these wonderful things for your partner, but there will be one or two ways of showing your love that will work like magic. (And if you're really smart, you'll learn what your love language is and make sure your partner learns it!)

- Never take your partner for granted. Express your love and gratitude regularly. Thank your partner for all the big and little things she does.

- Make time for each other. It's easy for long-term relationships to become stale if you forget why you enjoyed each other's company in the first place. Spend time together doing things you enjoy. Talk.

- Make love and be physically affectionate with each other. Intimacy is a big part of successful long-term relationships, and a healthy sex life will definitely keep your connection alive and exciting!

- Create rituals and reminders of your love. Write love notes, play "your song," have little code words, leave text messages for each other.

- Have interests and friends that are different from your partner's. This will enable you to bring fresh ideas, perspectives, and energy that can keep the relationship fresh and always expanding.

• Be your partner's biggest fan and best audience. Be supportive of him both inside and outside the relationship. Celebrate his wins and console him for his losses. Let him know that you are on his side.

• View any obstacles, problems, and challenges as opportunities for the two of you to learn and grow.

• Avoid threatening to end the relationship unless you experience an insurmountable problem. Unless your partner violates your strongest standards, commit to working out the problem together.

• Believe that you both were destined to be in this relationship. Look for ways to learn and grow in love together every day.

• Always treat your partner as well as you would like to be treated.

• Appreciate the fact that your relationship will continue to evolve and change over the years. Acknowledge the growth in yourself and your partner. Be willing to change. Make space for the new in your relationship while cherishing all that you have shared together.

Those whose relationships stand the test of time regard commitment as a chance to become masters of love and to find new ways to express their caring to a partner and to enrich the relationship. When problems arise—and they will—they hold the commitment they have made as more important than the problem, and they dedicate themselves to growing stronger together. True intimacy only becomes deeper the more we know and love our partners, especially when we are willing to give them the space to learn and grow and they give us the same.

The love we share at eighty will not be the same as the love we knew at twenty, but it can remain vibrant as long as we practice love consistently. Love is both an emotion and an action, and without one the other is worthless. You and your partner must feel love for each other and do loving things that keep the connection alive. That is the practice of the art of love.

CHAPTER 17

When the Going Gets Tough

Making a heavenly relationship takes a lot of very earthly work. Sometimes this is easy, but it can also be the hardest thing we ever do. While there can be immense delight, happiness, and contentment in a long-term relationship, there will also be heartache, disappointment, anger, misunderstanding, and pain.

Relationships are God's tools for polishing our rough edges, shining us up, and making us ready to go to an even higher level on the other side. Depending on the lessons we are meant to learn in this lifetime, we're most likely going to go through some difficult stretches, both personally and as a couple.

Sometimes our problems have origins that predate our current lifetimes. We could be working out karma that we created with our partner even before we were born. Occasionally when I read for couples, I'll pick up that they were together in a previous lifetime and the challenges that they are having are due to the way they treated each other then. If you have a sense that this might be true of your relationship, find someone who does past-life regressions and see what comes up. It could be that you are simply destined to go through this challenge for a period of time, after which things will smooth out when the karma is complete.

ACTIONS *Do Speak Louder than Words*

Most of us have good intentions when it comes to our relationships, but actions always speak louder than words. When there's a difference between what your partner says and how she behaves, believe the behavior. And when it's time to address problems, always use behavior as your basis for the conversation. It's very easy to have selective memory about the things we do or don't do. Your partner may protest, "I said I was going to be more careful about how I spend our money!" but if you produce a handful of credit card receipts for purchases on the Internet that your partner forgot to mention, you've made a pretty clear case for a problem that hasn't yet been addressed. Good intentions are all very well and good, but they can pave the road to a hellish relationship built not on trust but on unfulfilled commitments.

SPEAK *Up!*

Sometimes I wish everyone came with a label that says, "Handle With Care." It would remind us to treat each other mindfully. But that's not reality. What's real is that, whether we intend to or not, we will cause pain in our partner, who will hurt us too. When our ideas about relationships conflict with our partner's, or our feelings get hurt, we can become defensive. When we go through difficulties that our partners are not experiencing, they don't always understand how we feel. When kids or family or friends put demands on us, or when we confront illness, death, loss, or other tragedies, those stresses can push our relationships to the breaking point. This is why, when issues come up, you need to address them as soon as you can. This may not be comfortable, but it's the only way you can keep your relationship strong. Most of the time this is a process of getting clear about the issue, communicating with your partner, and reaching some kind of agreement as to what you both will do.

However, there is one significant exception: **if you feel your life, health, or safety is being threatened, don't hesitate to leave immediately.** These are not the kinds of problems that you should attempt to fix. Sometimes the most important karmic lesson for you to learn is when to get out, while your partner learns the lesson that actions have consequences. When the situation becomes critical and you feel you have exhausted all your options, you may have to take a stand and threaten to leave. But you have to be willing to walk out the door if things don't change. As I said earlier, you must clearly establish your standards and boundaries right from the start in your relationship, and if they are violated, you must take action.

However, if there is no threat and you find that stress, boredom, or some other reason has prompted a loss of love, you owe it to yourself and your partner to put in some work to try to heal the relationship. Remember, problems aren't necessarily a sign that the relationship is over—they may just be growing pains that you need to go through so you can become wiser and more loving. As I said earlier, often the worst thing you can do is to leave at the first sign of trouble, because you may be leaving behind a lesson you have to learn before you can make progress on the other side.

FOUR STEPS *to Help You Address Problems When They Arise*

1. Get clear about what's going on with you.

This step starts by knowing yourself and what you are like when you are emotionally healthy and balanced. You need to know your own energy well enough to figure out what's really bothering you, and why. What's throwing off your energy in the relationship? Why aren't your needs currently being met? What are your needs in this relationship? What's bugging you about your partner or the way things have been between you? Just saying, "I'm not happy" isn't clear enough—how could your partner respond to such a vague complaint? You need to be as specific as possible about what the problem is, how long it's been going on, what's causing you the most pain, and how your partner has not met your needs. How has he made you feel unloved or angry? You might consider seeing a therapist to become clear about exactly what's going on with your side of the relationship. Or you might talk with a friend who will agree to help you find clarity, rather than just commiserating. Or you might simply write down the answers to these questions on paper. Set up two columns: on one side, write, "What's okay with my relationship," and on the other, "What's not okay." Organize your thoughts as clearly as possible, because you will need clarity for your next step.

2. See what part, if any, you have played in creating or continuing the problem.

This step is not always easy. None of us likes to admit we're wrong or that we aren't being the perfect partner. And few of us want to believe that we would deliberately hurt someone we love, even when the evidence is right in front of us. We have to acknowledge our part in the problem and be part of the solution. Have you enabled your partner in any way? Did you fail to bring up the issue early enough, and now it's gotten out of hand? Is there part of your personality that is happy that this problem came up? (Sometimes when things are going too smoothly, people almost want to create a problem. It's as if they have to test the relationship. That comes from insecurity, either in the present relationship or something from your past.) It may be that you decide you bear no responsibility for this challenge, but you owe it to your partner to check.

3. Talk with your partner.

Communicate your concerns to your partner in a clear, nonaccusatory way. Do your best not to allow yourself to speak in anger or because you are upset. At the same time, this is not about negating the feelings that you have. You simply want to make sure that you can get your message across clearly without making your partner defensive, if at all possible. Give her the benefit of the doubt. Start your communication by stating your belief that she didn't mean to mess up or hurt you. To that end, don't say that *she's* messing up: speak about *your* experience. Instead of saying, "You always pick on me when we're out together and it makes me crazy!" you should say something like this: "Honey, when you criticize me in front of our friends, I get very upset. I feel like you don't think I'm good enough for you and that I'm failing you. It feels like you don't love me as much as you used to." Remember, denial is one of the most prevalent patterns in relationships, so you may not get the kind of response you are looking for from your partner. She sincerely may not know there is a problem. That's why expressing your own feelings is such an effective approach—she may deny there's a problem, but she cannot deny your feelings about the situation. (If she does, that's another story, and you need to get counseling to handle this, as it's probably a symptom of a larger issue.)

Once you've made your feelings clear, you can ask for what you would like instead: "Can you please be more careful when you're talking to me in front of other people? If there's something you feel you need to tell me to change or improve, I'm happy to hear about it, but I'd appreciate if you would do it in private. I would never criticize you in front of other people, and I am asking that you do the same for me." Notice that this is not about begging your partner to change, or saying that your needs are inconsequential. You are speaking from your experience, which is just as valid as hers, and asking her to honor you as her partner.

4. If things don't change, get help.

Sometimes you need an expert's knowledge to figure out where things are going wrong and to suggest options that you couldn't see otherwise. A good couples therapist will help you with techniques like role-playing, mirroring the behavior you hate, looking at issues from your respective families, and so on. We learn how to be in relationships from our parents, our families, and our past partners, and many of us have picked up some very dysfunctional patterns of behavior along the way. A therapist can help you uncover and change those patterns far more quickly than you could on your own. You may realize, for example, that your mother was always overly critical of you and that's why your partner's comments in front of others drive you crazy. Or maybe your father was always late for dinner because he stopped at the bar after work, and so you constantly worry when your spouse is late and doesn't call. Depending on the severity and extent of the problems, counseling or therapy might be a very helpful option for you and your partner, both separately as well as together.

The goal of therapy for you both is to process any issues, learn your lessons, and come to a higher place of loving energy. The thing to remember is that catching relationship issues early and addressing them will help you avoid having them threaten the relationship at a later point. If something is not right in your relationship, don't think, *We'll deal with this later.* Start working on making it better right now. However, the truth is that no counselor can help you or your partner unless you're both willing to help yourselves. You have to take responsibility for your part in the relationship and be willing to make changes to support your loved one. You have to be willing to compromise, be vulnerable, and forgive (three essential qualities in any relationship, as you'll see shortly). When you accept responsibility for your portion of a problem and agree to work on yourself, you are giving your partner permission to do the same.

Most importantly, you have to realize that you are the only one who can change yourself and that the same holds true for your partner. You are responsible for your half of the relationship. Your job, before you do anything else, is to make sure you are the healthiest human being you can be, so that you can love a partner in a healthy way. You must accept that your partner will be different from you, and as long as he has also done the work to be healthy and loving, then you both have done the best you can. Then, if the relationship continues, it will be the best you both can make it. If it does not continue, then it was time for you to move on.

Spotting TROUBLE

The best thing we can do for our relationships is to anticipate problems and come up with constructive ways to handle them in advance. Anticipation will help us weather the big and small storms that are inevitable in relationships and in life. To help you anticipate possible challenges, here are nine of the most common "hot buttons" in relationships, as well as ideas and suggestions for dealing with them if they arise.

1. Lies and dishonesty

Hopefully you eliminated any partners who lied to you long before you entered a committed relationship with them. But if you find that your partner has been concealing anything from you or lying to you, this is a major red flag. Sometimes people are afraid to tell the truth because they don't think they can be loved by anyone who knows their "secret." In some cases, the secret is minor, like the fact that they rarely trim their toenails or hate washing dishes or never balance the checkbook. In other cases the secret is something serious, like addiction, bankruptcy, a criminal conviction, or an earlier marriage. It's up to you to decide the proper course of action if you find that a partner has been lying to you, but if you do decide to stay together, I believe that counseling or therapy is a must for you both.

2. Jealousy

Every emotion, when taken to an extreme, can turn into something dark. When love is taken to an extreme it can become obsession, jealousy, and eventually hatred. Some people who are insecure in relationships will actually try to make their partner jealous. Others will become possessive, obsessing over their partner's every interaction outside of the relationship. Jealousy almost always has to do with a lack of self-esteem on the part of the jealous person. It can also signify a lack of trust. Jealous people either feel that they are not good enough for their partner and suspect that the partner is always looking for someone better, or they don't trust that anyone would be faithful in a relationship and guess that their partner is no different. The problem is that either of these assumptions can create the very behavior the jealous one is trying to prevent. If you have ever been with a jealous partner who is constantly checking up on you, asking where you were, who you were with, and questioning your truthfulness, you know how incredibly draining and alienating that energy is. And if you find yourself in the clutches of the "green-eyed monster," get help. Go to a counselor and make sure that your feelings have nothing to do with your own insecurities or unfounded fears.

3. Infidelity

The flip side of jealousy occurs when your fears and feelings have a basis in reality: that is, your partner is abusing your trust by seeing another person. Some people believe that any kind of infidelity should mean the end of a relationship, but I would hesitate to make a blanket statement like that. If your partner clearly knows that your rule is "one transgression and you're gone," that's one thing. But I've seen a lot of relationships and talked to a lot of people both here and on the other side, and that breadth of experience has given me a slightly different perspective. Sometimes we are drawn to another person because of past-life karma—it's an attraction we can't do anything about. It's our "Love Karma"—something we still need to work out in this lifetime. (It's also possible that your karma with your current partner is complete and both of you are ready to move on to someone else, which is why your partner is attracted to someone new.) However, although our attraction may be completely out of our control, the actions we elect to take because of it are not. And unless there has been some kind of clear understanding up front that both partners are free to see other people, infidelity for any reason always puts a strain on a relationship.

All too frequently, infidelity manifests as someone pursuing what is essentially a fantasy. Recently, I read for a married woman who was being pursued by a man she had known before her marriage. "You and your husband are good together, even though you're having the normal marital problems right now," I told her. "This other guy—you knew from day one his intent wasn't pure. But now there's a trickster energy trying to pull you away, and it's causing you to create a fantasy around this other man. Don't go after him—you'll regret it. You can get the romance back with your husband if you want to, but pursuing a fantasy with this other man will just bring you pain." How many relationships break up because one partner is dissatisfied and sees the "perfect" dream partner in someone who clearly isn't? And how many people leave a current relationship only to discover that the new partner is no more perfect than their previous one? If you feel that something is missing in your relationship, your first step should be to deal with it inside the relationship. Talk to your partner, go to counseling, and do the inner work to discover what's going on inside you that has tempted you to stray. In the course of this process, you may find that your current relationship is shaky because it, too, was based on a fantasy, and dealing with the real person you're with is a lot tougher than you had thought. It's up to you both to decide if you can make the relationship something that will fulfill you in the long term, or if you need to find new partners. But above all, make sure that your partnership is based not on fantasy but reality. Otherwise, you're going to keep going from partner to partner, always seeking something that may not exist.

Infidelity is an issue that you must deal with, because unforgiven infidelity is not something you want to have on your soul when you pass over to the other side. I've had too many spirits come through to me who cheated on their partners and are begging them for forgiveness. Not too long ago I did a reading for a woman whose former partner came through. "He cheated on you with more than one woman, and he made your life miserable and he knows it," I said. "But he had a lonely death because all these women left him. He says he deserved it, and he's on his knees because he wants to grow in heaven and he needs you to forgive him, even though he knows you can't." In almost every case, infidelity creates an enormous amount of pain both here and on the other side. If both partners do the work to get past the breach of trust, then even infidelity can be forgiven, but even in those instances, I would suggest that it not be forgotten—because the lessons learned are so important.

4. Work and competition

In many relationships today both partners work outside the home, and there can be tremendous stress in this area, especially if we spend a lot of our time at work. It's especially difficult if, as is happening more and more, our work takes us away from our partners for days, weeks, or months at a time. Most of us want to believe that our intimate relationship is one of the most important aspects of our lives, yet we may find greater happiness, recognition, and fulfillment at work. Conversely, we may have a great relationship at home but be completely stressed out on the job. If either of these is true, the intersection of our work life and home life can produce a lot of strain. Remember, to have a happy life—at work and at home—you need to put time, effort, and energy into your intimate relationship. Your partner needs to feel that she is one of the most important parts of your life, if not the most important, and far more important than any job.

In some relationships partners unconsciously compete with each other to be "the best": the best parent, the most successful money-earner, the best multitasker. In other cases one partner feels diminished by the other's success. But in relationships competition can be a cause of separation. I'm not talking about the friendly competition on a tennis court or in a game of Scrabble. If you are competing for success, or for recognition, or for the affection of your children, or over who makes the most money or has the most toys, you are not in a romance: you're in a sporting event where there will be winners and losers and it's all about keeping score. And as I've mentioned earlier in this book, keeping score is one sure way to kill a relationship. Relationships are about being a team, the two of you being able to do more together than you ever would do apart. You've got to put your energy into creating a great partnership and find ways to do things as a team. Spending time together, sharing rather than competing, and enjoying the simple pleasures of each other's company can keep your relationship strong. If you need to compete, do it at the office or find another tennis, golf, or Scrabble partner—or at the very least, make sure you let your intimate partner win occasionally!

5. Money troubles

Money can be a very divisive force in a relationship and is often a bone of contention for even the happiest couples. Who hasn't had an argument with a partner over money at some point? We've seen the negative effects of financial stress on many more couples than in past years, thanks to the recent global recession. In the United States there are even couples who want to get divorced but can't afford to. They can't sell their house, and they can't afford to rent another place so one spouse can move out, so they're forced to continue living in the same home even though their relationship is over. Other couples are forced to separate when one loses a job and moves to another city to find work. I've also seen far too many situations in which one partner has all the money and uses the power of the purse strings to control the relationship, or in which someone marries for money and security rather than for love.

If you're finding that you and your partner are arguing more and more often about money or that finances have become a major focus of your lives, you need to remember what brought you together in the first place. Many older couples I know talk with great fondness of their years of being young and poor together, when love was what really mattered and the fact that they were eating instant noodles and bottled spaghetti sauce every night was romantic. Indeed, I believe that one of the great benefits of the global recession is that it has made many people reassess the role that money plays in their lives. When things were good, many of us became fixated on material goods, but we are now discovering the pleasures of a simpler lifestyle. If money is an issue, get whatever counseling you need to put your finances in order, but remember what the Beatles sang so many years ago: "Money can't buy you love."

6. Sex

The biggest fights in a relationship tend to be over sex, money, religion, and politics. However, most people will tell you that if something's wrong in the bedroom, it can affect every other area of your lives together, and upsets with our partners can definitely affect our sex lives. If we're not connected sexually, a certain level of intimacy in the relationship disappears. Because most of us feel so closely connected with our partners during sex, if we are hiding something, it can affect our sex lives. I can't tell you how many women come to me and say the first sign they had that a partner was unfaithful was when he stopped wanting to have sex. Sometimes your sexual timing is off: your partner wants sex and you don't, or you get tired of doing all the initiating and would love your sweetie to make the first move for a change. Occasionally people will use sex or withholding sex as means of controlling a partner. Trying to "control" anyone is dangerous territory, especially when it comes to intimacy. By withholding sex, you are also withholding the opportunity to be close. A healthy, happy sexual relationship can keep a long-term partnership fresh and alive and help couples overcome minor disagreements.

The problem is that with commitment comes fidelity, and with fidelity comes familiarity, and then, God forbid, boredom—which is often the death knell for sex. It's a conundrum: having the same sexual partner over time allows you to know what your partner likes and doesn't like, how to turn him on, how she acts when she climaxes, and so on. Knowing your partner intimately can create incredible closeness. But some studies indicate that, biochemically, we are sexually attracted to the same person only for about two years. After that, sexual attraction is more mental than physical. The way to get around this diminishing of attraction is with variety. Human beings crave newness and surprise, especially when it comes to sensual pleasures. You may love chocolate, for example, but if the only chocolate you have is Hershey's Kisses day after day, eventually you're going to want Belgian chocolate, or English toffee, or even caramels. You need to be aware of the sexual temperature of your relationship and be willing to try different things to heat it up.

Often the best way to revitalize your sex life is to make sex a priority rather than an afterthought. Clear up any frustrations, doubts, fears, or other emotional garbage before you go to bed. Make time for sex, and focus on all of its beautiful, sensual aspects. Don't make it a rote "you do this, then I do that" performance. Pay attention to your partner. Laugh together—keep things light. Remember that this is supposed to be an expression of love between two people. Use your intuition—sometimes you'll be able to sense what your partner wants without being asked. On the other hand, you must be willing to ask for what you want and give your partner permission to do the same.

And be willing to experiment, to step out of your sexual comfort zone. My friend and colleague Malcolm Mills, who is also a tarot consultant, calls sex "playtime for adults," and he believes that pretty much any experimentation should be okay as long as you and your partner agree. So play out each other's fantasies. Try different positions. Put on naughty lingerie. Place a dirty phone call to your partner during the day. However, it is important that you are comfortable with your partner's sexual requests. If you are not comfortable, it's okay to say no. Sexual energy is one of the strongest forces in a relationship, and sometimes dark or trickster energies can come out in the bedroom. Listen to your intuition: is your partner's request for a particular kind of role-play just a desire for variety, or is there something darker going on?

Above all, if there's a problem in the bedroom, address it quickly. Many people are reluctant to talk about a sexual difficulty: they're ashamed, or don't know what's going on, or do know what's going on but don't want to share it with their partner. However, sexual issues can indicate problems in other parts of the relationship. If there are issues in the bedroom, the best thing you can do is to go to a therapist together. A professional may be able to help you both decide what healthy fun is and what may be an indication of a deeper issue that must be addressed. And remember, while sex is a vital part of any relationship, it's not a reason to stay in an unhappy one. Our sexual desire for our partner is guaranteed to wax and wane throughout the course of our relationship, and even in the most passionate partnership you can't have sex 24/7. Make sure the rest of your relationship is as strong, vital, and exciting as you want your sex life to be.

7. Children

Many of our long-term relationships involve children—the children you and your partner have together and/or the children you both bring to the relationship. Children shape your lives as a couple, probably more than any other factor. But all too often parents can neglect their relationship with each other because they feel the need to spend most of their time and energy with the kids. In many cases, especially when children are babies, they will require most of your attention. That's a natural part of the cycle of a relationship, but remember that your partner needs your love too. The best thing you can do for your kids is to care for them while you care for each other. My parents loved their children deeply, but all of us knew that their relationship with each other was just as important to them as we were. Make sure your partner knows that you haven't transferred all your love to the kids and that you still love him as much as you ever did. Happy relationships create harmony in the home and everyone benefits from it.

Your children will only be as happy as the two of you are together, so if you and your partner are miserable, staying together just for the kids is not a good idea. When my sister Alicia counsels couples with kids, she tells them, "I don't care if you're not 'in love' anymore—you owe it to your children to make it work and to heal your relationship for their sake. But if it's really not workable, children are better off in two happy homes than in one unhappy one. If the parents are miserable, their children will be miserable too." If you have children, it's your responsibility to do everything you can to support them while you work out things with your partner. If you end up separating, do everything you can to make it as easy on your kids as possible. And never, ever use your children as pawns in your relationship or as leverage to hurt a partner. That dishonors you, your partner, and your children and creates wounds that may take a lifetime to heal.

8. Outside influences

Outside influences, like family and friends, can affect our relationships deeply, in good ways and bad. On the positive side, loved ones outside the relationship can be the sounding boards and reality checks we need, the people we can go to for advice, clarity, or just plain letting off steam. If things are going haywire in your relationship and you feel you're losing it, it's really helpful to have a support system of friends and family who can tell you the truth. However, sometimes family and friends oppose your relationship for their own reasons: there may be differences in background, religion, financial status, and so on that make your friends and family uncomfortable. Or maybe they had a great relationship with your ex and disapprove of the replacement. Or perhaps they just don't like your partner (it happens—sometimes it's karma, sometimes it's just a difference in personalities). Alternatively, perhaps it's your partner's family and friends who just don't like *you*.

If family and friends on either side are creating division in your relationship, you'd better address it, because it will only continue to drain you and your partner. Here are some suggestions: First, you should know your energy and be clear if friends or family have affected it in a negative way. If you're usually a peaceful, happy person but find yourself unhappy or feeling chaotic whenever you're around family or friends, take note.

Second, you must set up an agreement with your partner as to how you both will interact with family and friends. If there are points of friction, you should acknowledge them and deal with them as best you can.

Third, when you and your partner disagree, settle the issue between the two of you—don't bring in "reinforcements" from the outside. I've seen too many relationships broken apart because partners have taken opposite sides in a friend's or family member's disagreement, or people outside the relationship sided with one partner in a disagreement.

Finally, listen to your friends and family and be open to their input, because they may see things that you don't. You may realize that what family and friends have to say is designed to help rather than tear you or your partner down, and that their suggestions are constructive and should be listened to. Check with your intuition and see if what they have to say rings true. If so, address it with your partner. If not, thank them for their caring and love, and get on with your life. Your relationship should be your priority: you and your partner should support each other first and foremost.

9. Loss or tragedy

The experience of tragedy and loss can really test a relationship. Illness, loss of a job, financial stress, a serious accident, death of family members—all can put almost unbearable strains on relationships. Most of us meet our partners in the good times, but we really get to know them when we see how they handle emergencies, crises, and stress.

Because so many people come to me after they lose a loved one, I see the effects of tragedy on relationships all the time. One couple recently lost their young daughter, and it drove them apart. Just being with each other reminded them of their child, and because they couldn't bear the sadness, they divorced. I've also seen couples grow closer and become stronger following tragedy. Once last year, a woman wrote me to ask for a reading for her sister and her sister's husband. The couple had lost their only son, Ronald, in a traffic accident and were having a hard time adjusting. The woman dreamed that her nephew came to her and said, "Contact Char, because I need to tell my mother that I'm okay." (He was a very determined spirit!) I was able to tell the couple that Ronald was fine on the other side. "You knew he wasn't going to be here long, didn't you?" I asked his mom.

"I always said to my husband that this child wasn't going to live a long life," she agreed. "It made me feel guilty when he was killed a week later."

"He's saying that he died because he had fulfilled his karma on earth," I told her. "He came to your sister in the dream because he wanted to make sure you and your husband were healed after this. He was a wonderful son, and he's happy in heaven, and he wants you to be happy, too."

So many couples tell me about horrible things they've had to endure—tragic accidents, deaths of children or other loved ones, business failures, serious disease—that caused them to become even closer. In times of trouble, couples either turn toward each other or turn away. There's a reason that some wedding vows include the phrases, "For better or worse, for richer or poorer, in sickness and in health." We are meant to support each other in good times, but especially when things get tough. If you can find the ways to stick together and grow through tragedy and loss, both you and your relationship can emerge from the pain stronger and better than ever.

CHAPTER 18

Intensive Care: Three Keys for Healing

Earlier in the book we discussed the qualities to look for when you make the commitment to a partner: trust, respect, truth, responsibility, friendship, the ability to give and receive, kindness, acceptance, and humor. We then talked about how to keep the relationship in balance when the going gets tough. But sometimes it seems that no matter how good we thought our partner was for us or how hard we try to work things out, our relationship seems to be irreparably broken.

Don't despair. Here are three keys to make it easier for you to overcome challenges and heal your relationship: compromise, vulnerability, and forgiveness.

Compromise

Whenever I speak with couples who have great relationships, the word that comes up the most is *compromise.* We must be willing to "give" on some things so we can "get" on others. Compromise also means celebrating our differences and allowing our partners to follow their own path. We each need space *and* closeness in a relationship. As Lebanese-American author and poet Kahlil Gibran once said, "Stand together yet not too near together." Although we are walking beside our partners, our journeys are always going to be slightly different. But our separate experiences can enrich the relationship, as long as we stay committed to coming back together and sharing what we have learned.

Vulnerability

A relationship is the place where we strive to be our best, but where we're vulnerable enough to be seen at our worst. All of us go through highs and lows, and knowing that we have a partner with whom we can be honest about our lows is an incredibly liberating feeling. You need to be willing to be vulnerable and open, to let a partner in and share your joys and fears. For some people, this kind of vulnerability is difficult to achieve, and it may take years for them to feel comfortable enough to be that honest. But shared vulnerability creates closeness between partners as nothing else does, and it is an opportunity to heal those parts of ourselves that need help. Vulnerability also means keeping an open heart with your partner, which allows him to be close to you. If you've been hurt in love before, it can be difficult to remember this in the rough times, when your partner may unintentionally reopen old wounds from previous relationships. But if you're willing to share your hurt and communicate clearly, you may find that your openness draws your partner closer and he will do his best to avoid hurting you again.

There is an old axiom that people admire us for our strengths but love us for our weaknesses. When you are vulnerable enough to show your "shadow side" to a partner, you'll feel a great sense of both commitment and freedom—you're so committed to the relationship that you feel free to let the unpleasant aspects of yourself come out. This doesn't mean you have permission to deliberately inflict your harshest emotions on a partner, but it does mean that if you're feeling angry or upset or depressed, you should feel certain enough in the relationship to share that fact with her. Vulnerability is admitting that we need help, that we're not perfect or even strong, and that we trust our partners to be there and assist us in our growth. It also means accepting our partners' flaws and weaknesses and that we will do what we can to help them.

Forgiveness

If there's one thing that will make a relationship last through time, it's the partners' ability to forgive each other. There are many types of forgiveness, and in a relationship you'll probably experience them all. There is forgiveness for thoughtlessness (she forgot to pick up the cake for your son's birthday), and forgiveness with a request to make amends (he bounced a check and you ask him to make sure there is money in the account the next time he writes one). There is forgiveness that you give without being asked (she didn't tell you about an important call, but you know she was hectically busy yesterday, so you let it go), forgiveness knowing that you'll probably have to forgive the same thing again and again (he never puts gas in the car), and so on.

Then there's forgiveness with the demand that the act *never* happen again. This is a tougher kind of forgiveness for you both to give and receive. I'm talking about forgiving someone after infidelity, violence, abuse, or financial malfeasance—something that threatens the very core of the relationship. Sometimes there are reasons to stay in a relationship even after it has been shaken in one of these ways. You may have children, there may be financial reasons or other practical considerations, or you may have moral or religious convictions that make it difficult for you to leave. Or it could be that your karma isn't done with this partner: there are still lessons you both have to learn in the relationship. Only you can decide if you can forgive a partner in this kind of situation, based on what is most important to you.

This is the most difficult kind of forgiveness, and it requires a lot of thought and probably many tears. However, you'd better be very clear that the reason you're staying is so significant that you are going to be willing and, more important, able to forgive. Is it possible to forgive after such an act? Yes—but with three caveats. First, you must stick to your demand that your partner never do such a thing again. I believe there need to be boundaries with forgiveness and consequences to behavior. You must make it clear that if your partner ever acts that way again, you will leave.

Second, and much harder, is that you must genuinely forgive your partner, let go, and move on. Remember that one of the principles of karmic justice is that as long as you learn your lesson and don't make the same mistake again you are free of that issue and can grow. If you don't learn from it, you will most likely repeat it. Unfortunately, unless we deal with our feelings surrounding our partner's mistake, we can find ourselves in the trap of making him pay for the same mistake again and again. That's why genuine forgiveness is so important. If you have unresolved anger, fear, or resentment regarding this issue, it will leak into your relationship and potentially damage it. Holding on to these emotions damages you as well as the relationship. (Resentment has been described as a poison that affects you rather than the one you resent.) If necessary, get counseling, either together or separately, to clear the air. It may take time for you to reach the point at which you can truly forgive your partner, but if you commit to working this issue through, your relationship can actually become stronger as a result, as long as both partners use it as an opportunity to learn and grow.

Third, you must forgive, but don't forget. All too often, abused women forgive their abusers because they think, *He'll never do that again.* In order to stay in the relationship, they do their best to forget—until the next time. This is the pattern of an enabler, and that's not the kind of forgiveness that produces healing and growth. A situation that demands forgiveness can be an opportunity to establish your ability to overcome a major problem in your relationship, and a warning to never let such a thing happen again. So forgive, let go of the emotion, but keep the act in your memory, a reminder of a boundary that must never be crossed again.

How about the times that you have to ask for forgiveness? Some of the hardest words to say are "I'm sorry, please forgive me." And sometimes you will probably need to apologize for things that were not a big deal to you but were to your partner! That's why being able to walk a mile in your partner's shoes is so important. Be willing to have the tough discussions and to discover the reason that your partner became upset. Hear her out fully, even if you think she's being unreasonable—*she* believes her reasons are valid, and you'll learn a lot more if you can listen without judgment. Once you've heard her out, do what you can to make things right.

Sometimes it can be tough to apologize if you don't really understand why your partner is so upset, especially if you know in your heart that you didn't mean to upset him. Intent is important, but so, too, is the effect of your words or behavior. A very thought-provoking question you need to ask yourself is "Which is more important: to be right or to be loving?" You can be right and self-righteous about it, but that will usually create distance between you and your partner. If you know your intent was good but the effect of your behavior on your partner was negative, one of the most effective ways to apologize is to say that you're sorry for how your actions made her feel. For example: "Sweetie, I'm so sorry that my siding with my mother when she was over for dinner made you feel like I loved Mom more than you. That was not my intent at all. I love you very much—you are the most important person in my life. Please forgive me." An effective apology has four key elements. First, it acknowledges your partner's feelings. Second, it expresses your love and commitment to the relationship. And third, it is a sincere request for forgiveness, not just a gesture to placate an upset or angry partner.

Of course, the fourth element of an effective apology is to learn from your mistakes and do your best not to repeat them. The next time Mom comes over, be aware that your partner may be hypersensitive to how you act around both of them. It doesn't mean that you have to treat Mom any differently, but if you're smart, you'll make clear to your partner how important your relationship is and how much love you share.

Equally important: forgive yourself! Too often we beat our-selves up for making a decision that didn't play out the way we wanted. Forgive yourself for any part you may have played in the problem. Learn from this experience for the next time love comes knocking at your door.

Learning Your LESSONS

Ultimately, the purpose of all our relationships is for both part-ners to learn and grow in our ability to give and receive love. Believe that you have chosen this partner, perhaps before you were born, to help you fulfill your purpose on earth. How you handle yourself in your relationship will determine whether you learn your lessons so that you can progress, or if you have to come back and learn them all over again with a new partner. This principle holds true on earth as well as in heaven, by the way. If you don't learn lessons about love, acceptance, stan-dards, forgiveness, compromise, compassion, trust, sharing, and respect with this partner, you'll take the same patterns with you into your next relationship on earth. Or you will take those patterns with you to the other side and will have to come back and learn them in a new lifetime. Yes, you will continue to repeat the same mistakes until you learn them, either here and now, or in another incarnation. It's part of the spiritual evo-lutionary process. The same is true for your partner. At some point, you both *will* learn these lessons, and you'll be ready to move on to another set of discoveries—perhaps with your cur-rent partner, perhaps with a new one. As psychiatrist and pio-neer in near-death studies Elisabeth Kübler-Ross wrote, "There are no mistakes, no coincidences. All events are blessings given to us to learn from."

I can't know what's in store for you in your long-term relationship. But what I do know is that any relationship is worth working on. All relationships have their ups and downs. Give your relationship a chance before you throw it away. See a marriage counselor. Do the necessary work, first on yourself, and then on the relationship. Do your best, and if it's right, you will stay with your partner, and the work you have done together will only make the relationship stronger—hopefully, strong enough to stand the test of time.

CHAPTER 19

Knowing When It's Over and How to Leave Graciously

You have that gut feeling . . . you *know* it's the right time to leave your partner, but you may or may not heed the signal that it's time for the relationship to end. Sometimes you get caught up in the drama of a fight and don't realize that you and your partner are going in circles, arguing without getting closer to resolving the conflict. Sometimes you don't even realize that you're giving so much energy to fixing the relationship that it's taking everything out of you. I see clients all the time who refuse to recognize the signs that the relationship is over. They're rearranging deck chairs on the *Titanic* while the ship's going down. In such cases, you need the assistance of others to point out what's going on and to suggest the correct course of action.

A Few Signs That It's Over

- You feel that you've given 110 percent and really made an effort to work on the relationship and you're still not happy.

- When you think about the relationship, you feel hopeless and helpless. Your intuition is telling you, "I don't deserve to be treated this way."

- You are committed to working on the relationship but your partner isn't, and you don't foresee any changes to this pattern in the future. Or your partner talks about changing but doesn't do anything. (Actions speak a lot louder than words.)

- You confront your partner with your feelings and get no response, or your partner negates your feelings in some way by not giving you the opportunity you want to communicate.

- You feel that either you or your partner is in denial about the problems in the relationship.

- You get a signal from the universe that makes you think it's time to leave. This can come in the form of a gut feeling, an intuitive warning, dreams, or even symbols, like seeing the license plate RUN123 or hearing the song "Born to Run" on the radio.

- You feel as if your partner is trying to control or manipulate you, using emotional blackmail, finances, or your children as weapons.

- You discover that your partner has been dishonest or has lied to you.

- You continue to hope things will work out, but you wake up in the middle of the night knowing that they won't.

- Your emotional or physical health, or the emotional or physical health of your partner or children, is being affected negatively by the relationship. I had a friend who was trying to talk with her partner about some serious issues. When he wouldn't listen, she lost her voice and had a hard time breathing— symptoms of an asthma attack. However, she had never had asthma before.

- You feel as if your partner is draining your energy.

- You feel as if you're losing yourself in this relationship— you don't feel like yourself anymore.

- Your partner typically resorts to anger, depression, or withdrawal if you want to talk about the relationship. Or you try to discuss matters and your partner completely refuses to talk or listen.

- You know that the alternative of being with this person is worse than being alone.

Even if *you* think the relationship can still be saved, you need to check if your partner has any or all of these symptoms; they should not be ignored.

One of the most important signs that it's time to leave a relationship is how you feel when you think about doing so. I once asked that of a client who told me that her marriage was on the rocks. "When you think about leaving him, what do you feel?" I asked. She thought a moment and answered with a sigh, "Relieved." Then she said, "A sense of peace."

It's natural to feel fear when you think about leaving—as the old saying goes, "Better the devil you know than the devil you don't know." But that's simply fear of change, along with a little inertia. It's certainly easier in some ways to stay put, but in the long run, all that will do is cause you more pain. If you've put in 110 percent and things still aren't working, better to walk away than stay stuck. When you're done and you know you're done, don't be weak or insecure and keep hanging on to the relationship. I know that giving up the dream of that one perfect relationship is hard, even if you know it's the right thing to do.

Human beings can find it difficult to acknowledge when they are outgrowing a relationship or need it to change. It's never easy to admit that this person whom we have loved no longer meets our needs. It's even more difficult to come to the realization that you fell in love with an image rather than reality or that your partner has changed in such a way that the relationship no longer supports either one of you. Don't feel you have to rush your decision, but be aware that postponing it may not do either of you any good. Often the most difficult time in a relationship is the time before we make the decision to stay or to go. Being on the fence is immensely painful. Once you decide either way, you'll usually feel a sense of relief. If you decide to leave and you feel at peace with your choice, then it's probably the best thing for you both. Above all, don't be too sad when a relationship ends. Instead, cherish the fact that this person shared your life for awhile. Then release this partner, and yourself, to find new love.

Ending a Relationship HEALTHFULLY and GRACIOUSLY

Ending a relationship is rarely easy or simple, but I do believe it can be done in ways that support you both. In any breakup there's usually one partner who wants to stay together more than the other, so there's hurt on at least one side. Things can get messy because someone's heart is going to be broken. It is true that one person will inevitably be hurt more than the other, but for the one breaking up it hurts as well. The hopes and dreams for a perfect relationship, and the good times that you shared, are gone for you both. Be aware that emotions will come up—hurt, rejection, abandonment, pain, loss, anger, and even relief—for you and your partner. Even the sanest partner can become slightly irrational at the end of a relationship. At times, people (including you) can obsess and argue over things like who gets the dog or visitation with the kids, or even who keeps the seashell collection from your first vacation. You need to start by committing to do your best to serve both parties' best interests. Only then do you stand a chance of ending your relationship healthfully and moving on quickly.

It's rare for both people to agree that a relationship is ending. Either one person or the other initiates the breakup, and depending on which you are—the one who wants to leave, or the one who is left—there will be different things that you can do to make the parting easier. Here are some observations and suggestions to help.

If You're the One Who Leaves

A therapist once told me, **"Clean cuts heal faster."** If you've ever been in a relationship where the breakup goes on and on, with one partner leaving and then coming back, I'll bet you found it really difficult. If you've decided to leave, you've done one of the most difficult things. Now, you owe it to your partner to end it cleanly if at all possible. Sometimes you have to love yourself and your partner enough to break it off so that you can both move out of the relationship and on to something better.

Honor your relationship by being as honest, clear, and compassionate as you can with your partner. Before you have "the talk," take a few moments to reflect on the relationship and the positive lessons you learned from it. That will put you in the best frame of mind to speak with your partner and be strong. Then sit down with your partner and say what you need to say. I suggest that you make it clear that your decision is made and the time for discussion is over. Your message is, "Thank you for all you've given me and it's time to move on." You should expect anger, tears, and other emotional responses depending upon how your partner typically deals with stress. Be firm and honest, and keep reiterating that you believe this is best for you both. Do not reward bad behavior by changing your mind if your partner becomes depressed, angry, or argumentative. Listen to what your partner has to say, but follow the guidance of your inner wisdom—logic, common sense, and intuition. This is a time when you will definitely need all three!

Sometimes a partner can have an intense and even irrational reaction to your decision to end the relationship. If you think this might be the case and you are worried at all for your personal safety, protect yourself. Have a friend present when you tell your partner that you are leaving. If necessary, announce the breakup via phone or even email. (*Normally I would consider this the coward's way out, but if you fear for your safety, then it is justified.*)

And beware of interpreting any communications from your partner as "signals" that you should get back together. You may still be closely attuned energetically, or trickster energy may be coming in to tempt you. This can be confusing. For example, you're in your kitchen, happy to be done with the relationship and ready to move on with your life, when all of a sudden "your song" comes on the radio. Right at that moment, your ex calls.

"I was just thinking about you: I have tickets to a concert of that group we like so much—you know, the one that sang 'our song.' I know we're no longer a couple, but would you like to go?" Major sign, right? Could it be that the relationship isn't really over? Don't be deceived—perhaps you and your ex just listen to the same programs on the radio. If you feel your decision to end the relationship is valid, and you've used logic, common sense, and intuition, don't let yourself be led down a path that you know will not serve you. You know you have worked hard and exhausted all chances for this to be a healthy relationship. Don't be lured by loneliness or what you had hoped your love would be. Make sure you're not getting caught up in the romance of being pursued. Let your inner wisdom keep you balanced and protected. Do the right thing, stick to your guns, and tell your ex goodbye.

Whenever you make the decision to leave, make sure to have a practical plan in place for what is going to happen afterward. Who's going to move out? When and how will you separate your bank accounts? How will you handle paying bills, visiting kids, and so on? Thinking this through in advance will (1) make leaving easier, and (2) show your partner that you are in earnest. Do what you can to make your breakup clean, and then your relationship can become a valuable memory instead of a painful scar.

If You're the One Who Is Left Behind

If you wanted to keep the relationship and your partner didn't, you will undoubtedly have more emotional work to process than if you were the one who left. While we all have our process, wasting years of your life because you refuse to let go makes no sense. You are putting your life on hold for someone with whom your relationship will never work out anyway. You need to figure out ways to handle your natural grief, hurt, anger, and other emotions so you can move on quickly.

However, be aware that your own biochemistry is going to make this transition difficult. Dr. Pat Allen, author of *Getting to I Do,* is a therapist with a very wise perspective on how to break up healthfully. She points out that women in particular have to break themselves of their literal addiction to a partner. Women link their elevated oxytocin levels, which create feelings of closeness and emotional bonding, to a partner's pheromones. Basically, every time we're around a partner or even in a place where he or she has left a scent, our oxytocin is triggered and we start to feel bonded again. When we break up with a partner, we go into oxytocin withdrawal, which can produce depression, anxiety, and neediness—all the classic symptoms of both drug addiction and a bad breakup. We continue to have our oxytocin triggered every time we are exposed to a partner's pheromones. Any kind of anchor to a partner, even the sound of his voice on the phone, can start the oxytocin cascade, and we spiral downward again into withdrawal. Eventually the link between the former partner and our oxytocin dwindles, but depending on the strength of the connection, it can take anywhere from *six months to two years* for it to disappear!

There are two reasons why it is so important to know about this oxytocin link. First, when you and your partner end the relationship, get everything of his out of your house. Clean everything top to bottom to get rid of his pheromones. Do not keep anything for sentiment's sake, or if you do, box it up and put it away for at least a year. Ask your partner not to call you or drop by. If you must see him, make the meeting short and stay away from him physically if you can. (I know, this sounds extreme, but it will help you get over your breakup much more quickly.)

Second, if you find yourself pining over your former partner even thought you know the breakup was best for you both, realize that it's not you—it's your oxytocin. It will be natural for you to feel sad and down until your body clears itself of the addiction. Similarly, if you see or talk with your ex and find yourself happy and excited, don't take this as a sign that you should get back together. Say to yourself, "I was on drugs, and my partner was the pusher," and do whatever it takes to bring yourself back to reality. I've told this information to several girlfriends who were going through rough breakups, and it's helped them immensely. Remember that your emotions are not always genuine—sometimes the way you feel is just a symptom of your hormones acting up. Stay strong in your convictions so you can move forward, not backward, and remember that this, too, shall pass.

When a relationship breaks up, you will undoubtedly deal with a ton of very practical details entailed by you or your partner moving out. Reach out to others for support—everyone from lawyers, accountants, and realtors to therapists, friends, and family. Make sure to take really, really good care of yourself. Call on one or two friends who will discuss matters with you: people who know the parties involved and can provide a shoulder to cry on, a sense of perspective, and a kick in the butt, if necessary. If you're in emotional pain, I strongly urge you to get counseling or some kind of professional help. This is not a time to be strong and think you should be doing this alone, or to be ashamed of the fact that you were "left." Feelings like rejection and abandonment are perfectly natural. Remember, however, that not all relationships work out, nor are they supposed to last forever. The goal of our relationships is to learn and grow from them. If you can do that, then your relationship has been successful, no matter how painful the breakup was. Let a good counselor or therapist help you heal faster and reach a point of recognizing the lessons so you can move on with your life, whether that means spending some time alone to regroup or getting busy with finding someone new.

Whether or not you choose to work with a counselor, I believe it's important to have some kind of ritual or process to mark the end of your relationship. Here is a version of classic release work. It is four easy steps that you can complete in a very short amount of time. However, once you start this process, please do all four steps. And if you feel too fragile to go through this, don't start until after you've seen a counselor.

STEP 1: Acknowledge what's lost.

This relationship is no more, and you need to declare that fact. This will prevent you from hoping that you'll get back together with your partner. You're done—say so. Say it out loud if that helps purge the emotion. Then write down a list in two columns: one for what you'll miss and the other for what you won't. It's good to be honest about what will no longer be in your life, the good AND the bad.

STEP 2: Look for the lessons.

What did you learn? Why was this relationship in your life? Even if the lesson is never to let yourself be attracted to that kind of person again, find something to learn from your experience. The clearer you are on the lessons, the easier it will be for you to move on.

STEP 3: Say goodbye.

This relationship is no longer a possibility. You're done, and so is your partner. Imagine she's moving to another country and you'll never see her again. You certainly will never see her in the same way again, so in a way, it's true.

STEP 4: Release your partner and yourself so you will be clear for a new relationship.

At the end of a relationship, I always suggest that people create some kind of release ceremony to mark the occasion. It's almost like a graduation or a memorial service, depending on your emotional state. We need to let go of what has been and clear our energy to prepare for something new. This ritual should be whatever you feel will work in your circumstances. I would suggest including a space-clearing exercise as one component of your ritual. It is easy to clear the energy in your home or apartment. Burn some sage or incense to change the vibrations. Light a candle, put a white light of protection around your space, and say to the universe, "I take back my power and ask my partner's energy to leave so we can both be free to achieve our highest good." Imagine every speck of your partner's energy leaving the space as you fill it with white light. Once you've cleared the space, say a prayer of gratitude to God or a higher power for giving you your freedom.

Above all, have faith that things happen for a reason and this parting was for the best. Sometimes our greatest gifts can come from the loss of a relationship. It can teach us lessons in humility and compassion. The pain and sadness we feel at the end of a relationship can open us up and make us more vulnerable. It's a chance for us to grow and learn and heal. It also means that something better may be coming down the road. Endings mean new beginnings. Of course, no one wants to be left behind by a loved one—but did you really want to be in a relationship where you weren't appreciated and loved the way you deserve to be?

Knowing when it's over and knowing when you're over it are two very different things. Eventually you will reach a point at which you no longer feel any attraction to your former partner. After that, assuming you are recovering healthfully, there will be a time when any pain or anger about the relationship is in the past. You may not want to be around your ex to be reminded of the problems you had, but you will be able to move ahead with your life and pursue other relationships.

At the next level, you can be around your ex without feeling much of anything—or perhaps you even think, *What did I ever see in her?* But there's another level: the point at which you can see your ex walking down the street arm in arm with someone else and not care—or even feel good that he has found someone new. This may take a little or a lot of time, and depending upon how long ago you broke up with a partner yourself, you may be thinking that you could never be so detached. But haven't you ever seen a boyfriend or girlfriend long after you broke up and been amazed that you had even liked the person? Or perhaps you still found them attractive but the pain of the breakup was so far in the past that you could barely remember it? If you are just now getting over someone, I hope that you get to that point sooner than you think you will. There is no more liberating feeling than wishing a former partner well because you are so whole and happy within yourself.

CHAPTER 20

The Big Cleanup: Moving On

As every cook knows, whether a meal is wonderful or dreadful, it's inevitably followed by the cleanup—not the most pleasant part of the process, but still essential. Likewise, when you end a relationship, there are things that need to be cleaned up, and this often means ongoing contact with your former partner. If you want to get over the relationship, do your best to keep such contact at a minimum, but keep it as cordial as possible. For any kind of property-related, financial, or legal issues, you might want to have a third party negotiate. However, unless your ex is being completely unreasonable, do everything you can to keep things civil. This will mean that you both can move on with your lives as quickly and with as little pain as possible.

If children are involved, civility is absolutely vital. If you and your partner have reached the point at which your relationship is broken, children are better off in two happy homes instead of one unhappy one. If the decision is to separate, be careful about how you discuss the decision and also how you speak of your partner. Children are very intuitive and they will pick up not just what you say but also your feelings. How you and your partner handle yourselves will influence the ways your children view their own relationships. Your relationship with your partner, and, if you decide to separate, how you conduct yourselves during and after that conflict, will shape the children's choice of partners and how they handle their own disputes and difficulties in the future. You both should do your best to be great role models for your children, who are the innocent parties in your breakup.

A very important step in leaving a relationship in a healthy way is to learn how to enjoy being on your own again. A friend of mine told me that he began to feel comfortable being single for the first time in years when he realized that he could stay in bed on a Saturday morning all by himself. You will eventually discover how to be comfortable with having just yourself for company. Here are a few tips for getting to that point:

- **Learn to treat yourself well for no reason other than your own worth.** You are valuable whether you are in a relationship or not. Acknowledge your self-worth, and use this time to develop new ways to appreciate yourself and your life.
- **Be courageous.** Take things that you thought might be difficult and find ways to enjoy them. If you haven't cooked for one in a long time, take a cooking class to help you learn how.

A therapist once told me the one thing that most people miss the most after a breakup is the companionship, not the sex.

- **Be proactive.** Look for new forms of companionship to enrich your life. You probably have an entire set of friends who knew you as part of a couple but not as an individual. You will need to develop a different kind of relationship with those friends, and some of them may side with your ex and avoid your company. This may be unpleasant, but it is natural. Use this as an opportunity to make new friends with whom you can go to movies, restaurants, sporting events, and other fun activities. You are establishing a new identity as a single person, and if you let it, this can be a time of great excitement, exploration, and fun.

- **Plan some fun escapes for yourself,** ones that have nothing to do with the old relationship and that get you into new activities or locations. If at all possible, avoid things that have strong memories linked to your ex: "your" restaurant, "your" favorite performer, the beach you used to visit together—why trigger all those old memories, both good and bad? Get out there and make new memories, by yourself and with other people. Do things that make you happy: not your former partner, not your kids—you. Develop new hobbies, or go back to the ones you may have left behind while you were in the relationship. Build a better life that goes beyond your old relationship. Become the person you were destined to be.

Soon—very soon, I hope—you should also be thinking about moving on and loving again. You should be comfortable with the time frame for moving on. Don't feel that you have to rush things, but don't wait too long, either. Sometimes you simply have to get yourself out there and date again even if you're still getting over your last relationship. It can be very tempting to sit at home and avoid meeting new possible partners, and if you're actively grieving the loss of the relationship, you're probably better off having fun with friends instead of dating. But for many of us, dating again can connect us to that part inside that wants to love and be loved in a healthful and happy way. Remember, you are never too (fill in the blank) to find love:

You're never too old, too young, too rich, too poor, have too many kids, have no kids, too busy, too lazy, too damaged to get back out there and find the person who is looking for *you* right this minute.

Go back to the beginning of this book and start the process of dating again, or at least start going out with your friends or attending social functions at your church, clubs, sports matches, and so on. Tune in to your intuitive sense again. Tell the universe that you learned your lessons and you're ready for a new love. (In fact, you're more ready than the last time because you've got more experience under your belt!)

Remember, the best gift we have is ourselves, and the more people you know and the more people whose lives you touch, the richer you will be in the truest sense of the word: rich in love, life, and laughter.

CHAPTER 21

Relationships Beyond Time: Love Never Dies

With all the difficulties that we can face in relationships, why do we still want them? Very simple: a great relationship is the closest thing to heaven on earth. Someone once said that God put us on earth to go two by two, and when we feel that we have found that partner—our "other half," our best companion— going through life becomes easier, happier, and more joyous.

When you have someone to share life with, the highs are higher, and the lows are easier to face. We can delight in each other's company and enjoy making memories together that will warm us both throughout our lives. Will there be rough spots? Of course—but if we come though them together, somehow our lives become richer as a result.

I see these kinds of loving partnerships all the time, between couples like my parents, my sisters and their husbands, and my friend Mary, who found her second husband, Harold, when she was in her forties and he was in his late fifties. Love is ageless and can occur at any time. Perhaps you've seen an elderly couple walking down the street, still holding hands after all these years. Or you have watched an older gentleman hold the door and tenderly help his wife enter a room. In them you can see a shining example of the beauty of a lifetime of love and devotion. But here's the real secret: whether your relationship is one year old or fifty, it doesn't matter, as long as your love is true and you both are committed to love and grow together. Love is the great joy of life, no matter how long it lasts on earth, because when we love truly, love lasts beyond death.

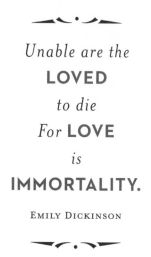

Unable are the **LOVED** *to die* *For* **LOVE** *is* **IMMORTALITY.**

Emily Dickinson

And sadly, that is one of the hardest lessons that we all must learn in the course of our relationships: While love lasts forever, life on earth does not. Each lifetime is short and often ends before we are ready to let it go. We may walk around as if we had all the time in the world to live, love, and give, ignoring the fact that we are here for a limited time and death is short-sighted. Even if we have the strongest, longest relationship we could ever wish for, eventually we must face the loss of our partner, or our partner must deal with our passing. Other than the death of a child, I believe the death of a beloved spouse is the most difficult parting a human being can face. To no longer see the beloved face or feel the caring touch we have cherished—the sense that our loved one is gone forever from our side—is a pain that increases with the amount of time we were together on earth. It's no wonder that for older couples, it's very common for one partner to follow the other in death within two years.

Some partners know that their time is coming and they do their best to prepare the loved ones they will leave behind. Even though he was only four years older, my father always told my mother, "You're going to outlive me and you need to be prepared for that." He didn't have any kind of health condition that made his death likely; he was intuitive enough to know that he'd go first, and he cared enough about my mom to give her advance warning. At other times people receive messages in their dreams, or they just have a feeling that something may happen, to themselves or to their partners.

Letting our loved ones go is one of the most difficult processes we will ever have to face. Whether it's making the decision to discontinue life support or simply letting go emotionally so that their soul can progress to the other side, we need to be brave enough to do what we believe our loved ones would want us to do. (And, I would add, smart enough for ourselves to make our preferences about end-of-life care clear before the end. Do your loved ones a favor and make sure you have something like a living will in place, so that if you are incapacitated and can't communicate, they can make decisions that are in alignment with your wishes.) Let their soul go. Give them permission to depart. Even if your loved one is taken in an accident or by a sudden physical cause like a heart attack or stroke, love them enough to tell them it's okay for them to leave. They will know that you have carried out their legacy, making it easier for them to feel peace. Giving them your blessing allows them to step gently over to the other side without lingering emotional trauma or negative energy. Know that your beloved ones are surrounded by love and light. All their pain is gone, left behind with their physical body. Loved ones who have passed over before them are welcoming them. And your loved ones will do the same for you when it's your turn to cross over. It is a reunion to be looked forward to with joy.

Even amid the pain of losing a beloved spouse, know that our loving relationships do not disappear with death. Love never dies: it is the bridge between this world and the next. Your love for your partner will keep you connected for eternity. Indeed, it is the conduit you and your partner can continue to use to connect earth and heaven. So many people tell me that even after a loved one has departed, they can still feel the person's presence. They'll enter a room and have a strong sense of their loved one's energy, or they'll catch a movement out of the corner of their eye and know that their partner is around. One of the most frequent ways our loved ones communicate is through our dreams, so I always suggest people keep pencil and paper by their beds in case a message comes through during the night. Sometimes we'll get clear signs and signals, such as lights that flicker on and off for no reason, or things that move or suddenly appear. (One woman reported looking for her sunglasses in order to wear them to her husband's funeral. She went into the closet and a shoebox fell on her head. When she opened the box, there were her sunglasses.) Perhaps we keep hearing "our song" played on the radio, or we see objects or animals that symbolize our partner. One man reported seeing a white butterfly on top of his wife's grave every time he went there—butterflies are a frequent symbol used by our loved ones to let us know that they are free. These are signs that our loved ones are letting us know they are still with us. Sometimes we'll get a sign that will help us find our missing keys or simply as a reminder to us that love never dies.

It's also possible that it might take a while for your loved one to come through. Death is a great transition, and it takes a while for the soul to become accustomed to its new state. In the same way that we must get used to not having the physical presence of our loved ones in our lives, they must get used to relating to us in a new way. Give them their space; don't wish them back or hold on to them too strongly. Souls have work to do on the other side: they continue to learn and grow, and they can be hampered by our desire to keep them with us. They are held back by neediness and excessive grief and sorrow. In the same way, the strength of our emotions or our desire to communicate with a departed loved one actually can get in the way of their communication.

I remember clearly one woman whose daughter brought her to me for a reading. Marie had lost her husband seven years earlier. Marie said she didn't believe in the afterlife, but she wondered if her husband's spirit was alive somewhere and knew about the grandson that had been born after his death. "Your husband's name was Mart, yes? He says he's visited you in dreams and given you other signs, but you don't really believe in communication with spirits," I told her. "You have no faith. In fact, you're still angry that he died. Your daughter's having dreams about him and she even tells you about them, but you won't listen. You even woke up at night and thought he was next to you in the bed and went to touch him. You're so mad at him for dying that you won't allow yourself the option to believe. It's time to let him go and change the way you think about him. Imagine him as being happy and having a great time on the other side. That's what he wants for you, your daughter, and her son."

Let your loved ones go and wish them well on the other side, knowing that their love for you is eternal. Their spirits will be waiting to receive you when you pass over, ready to welcome you and make you feel at home. Know that they are with you forever, and that all you need to do to communicate with them is to bring them to mind and send your loving thoughts their way. Your love and prayers are a bridge to the other side, and they will keep your relationship with your partner loving and vital until you see each other again.

Love NEVER *Dies*

The bond between you and a loving partner is eternal and will last even after the great transition of death. But that does not mean you should close yourself off from other loving partners in the future. Your departed partner doesn't want to be your only source of love—that would be selfish and cruel. From that eternal perspective, your partner recognizes that you have more love to experience for as long as you live, and to close yourself off from love would be a great tragedy. The best tribute you can make to your departed loved one is sharing your love with those who are still here. Stay connected with the dear ones who have passed over—feel their presence, wish them well, ask them to watch over you and be with you always. Thank them for the love they shared with you on earth and for the eternal love they have for you still. Then turn around and give your love to the people who are here on earth. That is what our loved ones want for us, and the greatest gift we can give them on the other side.

Sharing our love with the people around us may take the form of another intimate partner, or it may not. When my father died, my mother was only sixty-nine years old and a wonderful, loving soul. She also was still very attractive. There were many men in her circle of friends who would have been delighted to date her, but she wasn't interested. It wasn't because she was so devastated by my dad's death that she couldn't love again. She simply felt that she had had the love of her life for forty-six years and now she was at peace with being by herself. Especially when people have been in a very long and close relationship, they may not want to find someone new, and that's just fine. As I mentioned earlier, their karma in this lifetime may have been to have one relationship. However, it's equally fine for someone who has lost a spouse to death to date and even marry again. My cousin lost her husband to cancer when he was fifty years old. She later met on a widow/widower's website a man who had lost his wife to cancer when *she* was fifty years old. They ended up marrying and today they're both deeply happy. Their lives are very different than they were during their first marriages, but it's clear they were meant to be together.

Some people who lose a spouse close themselves off from new love because the loss of the old one was so painful. Or they can feel guilty dating someone new, almost as if they were "cheating" on their deceased spouse. However, love isn't exclusive, and someone who remarries isn't being unfaithful to the dead. If the person you love dies, your love for her can continue, and she will feel your love from the other side. But that doesn't prevent you from loving someone new. If you had a good relationship with your deceased spouse, then you know how to love and be loved, you know how to care for someone, and you know how to be a loving partner. Why *wouldn't* you share that gift with someone else for the years you are on earth?

I can assure you that our departed loved ones want us to feel love while we're here. When they speak through me, they usually urge their partners on this side to move on and love again. And they are often delighted to see that the wife or husband or partner that they cared so much about is happy in a new relationship. Not too long ago, I saw quite an unusual demonstration of this on one of my TV shows. Inge had been married to Adrian, a wonderful man, for five years before he got cancer. She nursed him throughout his illness and was with him when he died. Adrian's brother, Jan, comforted Inge, and eventually they fell in love and married, only to have Jan, too, get cancer and pass over.

Both men came through to speak with Inge that day. "Jan is your second husband, right?" I asked her. "He's saying that one of the reasons he fell in love with you was that you were so empathetic and caring for his brother, and he wanted the same unconditional love. It's the reason he married you, because somewhere deep inside he knew that he would be sick, too. Did he tell you this?"

"Jan didn't, but my first husband, Adrian, did," Inge told me. "Adrian said to me that it would be better when he passed away, and that I would live with Jan. I told him that was ridiculous, and I asked him why. And he said, 'Never mind—you won't be with him long either.' Afterward I understood what he meant."

"Well, Adrian has another message for you now. He says that you're going to have another romance." I had to laugh. "He's saying, 'I'm a better psychic than Char, because I told you about Jan and now I'm telling you about a new man!'"

Adrian is typical of most of the spirits I speak with who have partners still on earth. They really want the best for their loved ones and encourage them to leave their grief behind and to move on and find new love. Because they have passed over, they know with much more clarity that love never dies, that our loving connections with each other remain even after death, and that new love only adds to our lives and does not diminish the love we had (and still have) for them. They know that everyone deserves the greatest amount of love while here on earth, as well as on the other side. If you have lost a spouse, never feel that you beloved wouldn't want you to find a new love to be with while you're here.

There is a reason that wedding vows include the phrase "until death do us part." While your love forms a bridge that crosses over to the other side, your relationship with your loved one will be changed by death. Your love for them may not diminish, but it will change. You should be open to a new love on this side for the years you are still here.

Life is for the living. If the person you love dies, your love can continue—but that doesn't mean you can't have a different love for someone else. If necessary, work through this issue with a counselor so that you can feel truly free to love again. And should you have any uncertainty about this fact, ask your departed loved one directly. Be aware that sometimes the dead will not readily give their blessing. And if that is the case, make the decision to pursue or not to pursue the new relationship based on common sense and your own intuition: your "inside knowledge from your wisest self."

CONNECTING TO OUR LOVED ONES ON THE OTHER SIDE

Close your eyes and put a white light of protection around yourself. Call to your departed loved one and ask him to give you his blessing to be in a new relationship. Be aware, however, that we keep our personalities when we pass over. If your spouse was negative or controlling or jealous, it's possible that he may not be ready for you to find someone new. In this case, your karmic lesson may be to stand up for yourself and pursue the new relationship anyway. If you really want to love again, you should feel free to do just that. Send good thoughts to your former spouse and wish that he will learn and grow on the other side in ways he wasn't able to on earth.

And if you have a parent, sibling, or friend whose partner has died and who finds a new love, please be open to accepting her choice. I've seen many great relationships stressed or even destroyed by the disapproval of friends and family. Certainly, listen to your inner wisdom, and if you believe someone is rushing unwisely into a new relationship out of loneliness or desperation or an inability to be alone, make your concerns known. But love is important—do not prevent someone from sharing it because of your own fears or even jealousy. Trust that the universe will care for your loved one, and do your best to help her find the love she is seeking in a new partner.

CHAPTER 22

All You Need Is Love: A Truly Heavenly Relationship

The purpose of being in any relationship—indeed, our purpose for being born—is to learn and grow in our ability to give and receive love. We choose our relationships for the lessons we can learn from them, and how well we learn those lessons will determine how we progress on the other side.

Your lesson may be to love one partner for fifty years, or to have several partners, each of whom will come into your life to teach you a different lesson. In the same way, you may have profound lessons to share with the partners who come into your life. Ultimately, however, our deepest relationship is not with our intimate partners, our children, or even ourselves.

Our deepest relationship, the one that is the source of every other love, is our soul's relationship with what I call *Essence*. It is the core of goodness, wisdom, love, and compassion, and its energy composes the universe. We are part of Essence and it is part of us. Within each of us is a pattern of perfection, and as we go through the lessons of each lifetime we grow closer and closer to being one with perfection—one with Essence. To that end, we naturally attract exactly the people and the experiences we need to grow and learn in love.

It's up to us how well—and how quickly—we learn those lessons, and how much love we share with other souls who are on the same journey. Remember, our soul mate is someone who helps our soul to grow.

Our intimate relationships are designed to teach us about Essence in its most tangible and easy-to-understand form: that of love between human beings. While we love our partners here, only on the other side will we see them as they really are. Only then can we clearly see the pattern of our lives and the purpose we each have served and how we have served them. At that point, we will understand the journey we have taken together, why we have gone through the joys and pain of this lifetime, how we have grown together, and most importantly, how we are all reflections of the perfection of divine love. We'll see the role our partners have played in our lives and how they helped us learn and grow, as we have done for them. We'll see our mistakes, too, and the lessons we will need to learn more fully in the next life. We'll understand that our intimate partners came into our lives to be our greatest teachers, as we became theirs.

As spiritual teacher Byron Katie wrote, "People go to India to find a guru, but you don't have to: You're living with one.

Your partner will give you everything you need for your own freedom."

If there is one lesson that divine love wants us to learn, it is this: *Never be afraid to jump into love again.* **Never let fear or hurt or anger or discouragement stop you from seeking and finding a new partner.** Your love is a gift that you were born to share with a soul mate, with friends, with family, and with partners who will teach you how and how not to love. You have so much to give and to receive from others: your love is a force that can uplift other human beings and transform their lives, and they can transform yours.

You may have had the gift of a long and happy intimate relationship, or you may have experienced great pain from one. Or you may have had many relationships, or, for whatever reason, you may never have had the relationship you wanted in this lifetime. It doesn't matter. Be grateful for every occasion you have been able to give and share your love with another person.

May you recognize divine love in a partner whom the universe has sent to hold your hand throughout your life. May you learn and grow in giving and receiving love with every partner, every relationship, and every minute. May your love be the spark that makes someone else light up when you walk into a room, and may you feel that same spark inside. Most of all, may you always remember that our purpose here and on the other side is to know the divinity of love wherever we see it: in ourselves, in our partners, in our families, our friends, and in the goodness of this world and the next. May your journey of heavenly relationships bring you great love and great joy.

INDEX